NOTES ON ARCHITECTURE

Crisp Publications, Inc.

95 First Street

Los Altos, California 94022

Library of Congress Cataloging in Publication Data

Main entry under title:

Notes on architecture.

  Bibliography: p.
  1. Architectures—Handbooks, manuals, etc.
I. Hanks, Kurt, 1947-
NA2540.N67   1981   720   81-17205
ISBN 0-86576-022-5 (pbk.)   AACR2

ISBN 1-56052-057-4

This book was created atInformation Design, Inc. It was produced through the joint efforts of the following:

Larry Belliston - Developer/Planner
Kurt Hanks - Director
Jay A. Parry - Editor/Writer
David Bartholomew - Production Artist
Scott Bevan - Illustrator
Jill Moffat - Typographer
Michael V. Lee - Technical Consultant

Readers who wish additional information or who have other suggestions for changes, and/or other improvements are invited to write to the publishers who will appreciate any material and will share it with the authors.

INTRODUCTION

■ These notes on architecture represent more than fifty years of combined professional work in the field. During that period we have personally designed and supervised the construction of numerous buildings. We have taught many "apprentices" of the art of architecture, helping them with their own design projects. This combination of experience has compounded our understanding of architectural principles many times over.

■ An understanding of those principles is vital to success in architecture. Skills are essential, of course, but a basic understanding must come first. Everything you ever do in architecture will stem from the principles you learn as a student. Principles will tell you how things work; they will tell you how to *make* things work. *All truly successful professionals in the field can attribute their success to a thorough comprehension of the fundamental principles of architecture.*

■ These are the reasons why we've emphasized *principles* in these notes. Our purpose is not simply to give you facts; you can get those elsewhere. Instead we seek to give you that crucial basic understanding.

■ A quick flip-through will show you that this book is highly visual. We don't just *tell* you about architecture; We *show* you about it as well. Since architecture is a highly visual field, the best way to communicate it is through visual means.

■ It has often been said: A picture is worth a thousand words. Add up all the pictures in these notes, each one carefully chosen, multiply the number of pictures times 1,000 words, and you'll find that you have the equivalent of a very fat book here!

■ We don't intend to get into theory—the deep, dark secrets of what architecture means. We're simply giving you a place to start. Only after you've mastered the ideas and principles in these notes will you be ready to move on to a deeper understanding. Serious students will be able to take those ideas and build on them until they are true professionals in the field.

■ *Use* this book with care and you'll find that your understanding of this truly exciting subject of architecture is progressing at an exciting rate!

CONTENTS

ARCHITECTURE

arch \ ärch\ *n* [ME *arche*, fr. OF, fr. (assumed) VL *arca*, fr. L

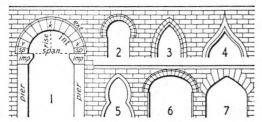

arches 1: *1* round: *imp* impost, *sp* springer, *v* voussoir, *k* keystone, *ext* extrados, *int* intrados; *2* horseshoe; *3* lancet; *4* ogee; *5* trefoil; *6* basket-handle; *7* Tudor

arcus — more at ARROW] **1** : a typically curved structural member spanning an opening and serving as a support (as for the wall or other weight above the opening) **2 a** : something resembling an arch in form or function; *esp* : either of two vaulted portions of the bony structure of the foot that impart elasticity to it **b** : a curvature having the form of an arch **3** : ARCHWAY
²arch *vt* **1** : to cover or provide with an arch **2** : to form or bend into an arch ~ *vi* **1** : to form an arch **2** : to take an arch-shaped course
³arch *adj* [*arch*-] **1** : PRINCIPAL, CHIEF ⟨an *arch*-villain⟩ **2** [*arch*- (as in *archrogue*)] **a** : cleverly sly and alert **b** : playfully saucy
arch- *prefix* [ME *arche*-, *arch*-, fr. OE & OF; OE *arce*-, fr. LL *arch*- & L *archi*-; OF *arch*-, fr. LL *arch*- & L *archi*-, fr. Gk *arch*-, *archi*-, fr. *archein* to begin, rule; akin to Gk *archē* beginning, rule, *archos* ruler] **1** : chief : principal ⟨*arch*enemy⟩ **2** : extreme : most fully embodying the qualities of his or its kind ⟨*arch*rogue⟩
¹-arch \ärk, *in a few words also* ərk\ *n comb form* [ME *-arche*, fr. OF & LL & L; OF *-arche*, LL *-archa*, fr. L *-arches*, *-archus*, fr. Gk *-archēs*, *-archos*, fr. *archein*] : ruler : leader ⟨matri*arch*⟩
²-arch \ärk\ *adj comb form* [prob. fr. G, fr. Gk *archē* beginning] : having (such) a point or (so many) points of origin ⟨end*arch*⟩
ar·chi·tect \'är-kə-,tekt\ *n* [MF *architecte*, fr. L *architectus*, fr. Gk *architektōn* master builder, fr. *archi*- + *tektōn* builder, carpenter] **1** : one who designs buildings and superintends their construction **2** : one who plans and achieves a difficult objective
ar·chi·tec·ton·ic \,är-kə-,tek-'tän-ik\ *adj* [L *architectonicus*, fr. Gk *architektonikos*, fr. *architektōn*] **1** : of, relating to, or according with the principles of architecture : ARCHITECTURAL **2** : resembling architecture in structure or organization — ar·chi·tec·ton·i·cal·ly \-i-k(ə-)lē\ *adv*
ar·chi·tec·ton·ics \-'tän-iks\ *n pl but sing or pl in constr, also* ar·chi·tec·ton·ic \-ik\ **1** : the science of architecture **2 a** : the structural design of an entity **b** : system of structure
ar·chi·tec·tur·al \,är-kə-'tek-chə-rəl, -'tek-shrəl\ *adj* : of, relating to, or conforming to the rules of architecture — ar·chi·tec·tur·al·ly \-ē\ *adv*
ar·chi·tec·ture \'är-kə-,tek-chər\ *n* **1** : the art or science of building; *specif* : the art or practice of designing and building structures and esp. habitable ones **2** : formation or construction as or as if as the result of conscious act **3** : architectural product or work **4** : a method or style of building

KEY POINTS ON ARCHITECTURE

- The practice of architecture includes defining problems, evaluating alternatives, and implementing solutions.

ARCHITECTURE

- It involves forging effective compromises between divergent demands, and it means setting priorities by determining relevancy.

- It requires a fusion of interconnected and interrelated areas. When one area is affected, all others are likewise affected.

- It takes on different forms, depending on its physical, historical, and cultural environment. The purpose of architecture is to produce an aesthetically pleasing structure within functional restraints.

- It is built on a historical framework which has been evolving from the beginning of civilization.

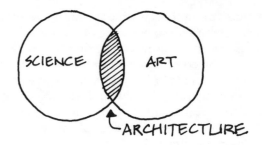

- It is both an art and a science. As a science, architecture must produce structures that are well planned, strong, and practical. As an art, it must produce structures that are aesthetically pleasing.

- It evolves as mankind's cultural expectations and technological innovations evolve.

- It can be a political tool for social symbolism.

- It must be experienced to be valid; each person reacts to a particular design in a unique way.

- It is a critical element in the field of design, Architecture encompasses and works with all other aspects of design.

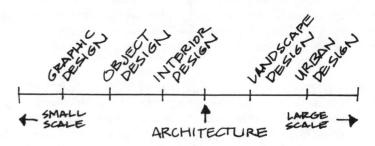

- It is a human activity that must make humane decisions.

- It is one of the fine arts.

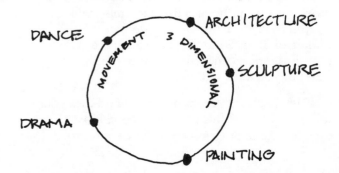

- It protects life, promotes health, safeguards property, and enhances public welfare.

- It is *used* by living human beings, with all their needs, wants, habits, frailties, and inconsistencies. The success of an architect's work can be judged only within the human context.

KEY POINTS ON THE ARCHITECT

■ An architect's goal is the synthesis of a multitude of diverse elements into a cohesive, structural whole. He or she takes abstract ideas and symbols and helps turn them into real form. An architect solves problems.

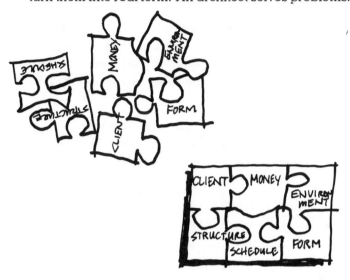

THE ARCHITECT

■ Organizes the form of the human environment.

■ Must work within environmental and human constraints to create a building in its total context.

■ Must work with the economic process, creating economic designs to match economic solutions.

■ Must work under imposed financial limits, still finding optimal building solutions.

■ Must use environmentally sound approaches to planning and development.

■ Must be farsighted: his or her structure will continue for many years into the future.

■ Works with and is often the team leader of many or all of the following:

- Contractors
- Engineers
- Urban and regional planners
- Interior designers
- Industrial designers
- Landscape architects
- Color and lighting experts
- Electricians
- Carpenters
- Draftsmen
- Surveyors
- Architectural representatives
- Corporate officers
- Field inspectors
- Delineators
- Artists
- Graphic artists
- Specification writers
- Computer graphics technicians
- (add your own names to this list)

■ Must have a wide range of qualities, including:
- drawing and sketching ability
- ability to visualize entire buildings
- understanding of the building process
- knowledge of materials and their forms and functions
- a good head for details
- a good sense of spacial perspective
- a sense of appropriateness
- scientific and mathematical ability
- persistence
- ability to work under pressure
- ability to get along with other people
- ability to supervise others
- a good imagination

■ Must have the point of view of a generalist and the expertise of a specialist.

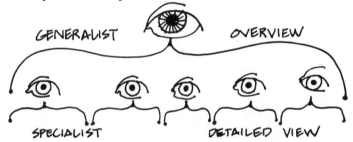

QUOTES ON ARCHITECTURE

"Architecture is a discipline, a profession, and a state of mind."

—Anthony C. Antoniades

"Architecture has its political use; public buildings being the ornament of a country; it establishes a nation, draws people and commerce; makes people love their native country. . . ."

—Sir Christopher Wren

"A building must meet the following standards to qualify as architecture: it must conveniently serve the purpose for which it was built; it must be structurally sound; and it must be beautiful."

—Marcus Vitruvius Pollio

"A building serves three purposes: to meet the social and economic needs of living, to delight the senses, and, last but not least, to symbolize all that men aspire to hold and to command."

—George Howe

"Good architecture is always a perfect expression of the time in which it is built, not only of that time's artistic skill but also, if it is interpreted correctly, of its religion, its government, even of its economic and political theories."

—Talbot Faulkner Hamlin

HISTORY

■ Today's structures are determined by yesterday's architecture. It's impossible to make a workable and pleasing building design without some awareness of what has gone before.

■ The following brief survey touches on major architectural styles and periods of the past and present, including specific examples throughout, and it ends with a look toward the future.

EGYPTIAN 2000 B.C. to 100 B.C. The earliest influence on European architecture. *Temple of Karnak, Ziggurat of Sakkara.*

■ Knowledge of mathematics and astronomy
■ Aesthetic and religious concerns
■ Plants—papyrus and lotus influenced column orders
■ Imposing display of facades, multi-columned courts, and walls covered with picture writing
■ Repetition—a symbol of stability and permanance

AEGEAN 2000 B.C. to 1275 A.D. Known as "Archaic" or "Minoan." *Palace of Minos, Knossos, Crete; The Treasury of Atreus, Mycenae.*

■ Spontaneous style—structures designed as they were built
■ Large rough stones and colorful wall paintings
■ Cylopean—massive structures (as if constructed by giants for giants)
■ Middle eastern influence in details but not in design
■ Without geometry (a labyrinth)

GREEK 1100 B.C. to 350 B.C. *The Parthenon, Propylaea, Temple of Victory, Erechtheum, Theatre of Herodes Atticus; Acropolis, Athens.*

■ Buildings mostly rectangular
■ Porches supported by columns to create shaded walks
■ Sensitive site selection
■ Harmony between building and natural materials

DORIC 900 B.C. Simple structures standing directly on the ground. Ribbed shafts, no ornamentation on top. Brightly painted. Often stocky in appearance.

IONIC 600 B.C. Rich carvings important. Narrow shafts usually standing on a pedestal. Double scroll at top.

CORINTHIAN 400 B.C. Carvings were often representations of the acanthus, a leaved thistle that lends itself to stylization. Ionic scrolls were used above the thistle garlands. Corinthian links the Antique and Hellenistic periods.

ROMAN 150 B.C. to 1000 A.D. *The Pantheon, Arch of Titus, Basilica of Maxentius, Porta Maggiore, Rome.*

■ Dome, the arch (which often followed free-standing columns)
■ Basilica—an aisled assembly hall with a vaulted, semi-circular room at one end.
■ Pillar and arch construction, barrel vaulting and cupolas
■ Sites made to fit the buildings
■ Circular buildings spanned by domes

BYZANTINE 500 to 1000 A.D. *Church of Santa Sophia, Constantinople, St. Paolo-outside-the-walls, Rome, St. Vitale in Ravenna.*

■ Early Christian style influenced by Roman and Oriental styles.
■ Oriental motifs used for decoration
■ Smaller churches built—well ornamented
■ Mosaics and murals of religious events predominant in ornamentation
■ Centrally focused ground plan

ROMANESQUE 1000 to 1200 A.D. *Worms Cathedral; St. Zeno, Verona; St. Miniato, Florence.*

■ Thought of as the first Western European style
■ Continued use of the basilica, with the addition of towers
■ An elevated choir
■ Cruciform (a vault in the shape of a cross)
■ Antique, Oriental, Byzantine, and Nordic styles all important influences

ISLAMIC 740 to 1480 A.D. *The Great Mosque, Cordoba, Spain; Sultan Hassan Mosque, Cairo.*

■ Influenced by Byzantine style, church of Santa Sophia used as partial model for mosques
■ All possible styles of arches, vaults used
■ Intricately carved ornamentaion with no human forms represented
■ Stucco walls and ceramic floors common
■ Minaret (prayer tower) important Islamic element

GOTHIC 1150 to 1520 A.D. *Cologne Cathedral; Notre Dame, Paris; Strasbourg Cathedral; Westminster Abbey, London.*

- Tracery, rose windows
- Large windows and columns (rather than traditional walls) allowed much natural light inside the structure
- Flying buttresses and pointed arches used extensively
- Ground plan based on a five-aisle space with some aisles half-encircling the choir
- Walls required extra support because of their unique nature
- Gothic was popular in England, France, Germany, and Italy.

RENAISSANCE 1420 to 1600 A.D. *San Zaccaria, Venice, Italy, Strozzi palace, Florence, Palazzo Farnese, Rome.*

- Use of Golden Section to insure absolute beauty
- Began in Italy—strongly influenced by Greek and Roman styles.
- Centralized buildings, solid facades, strong walls (eliminating buttresses)
- Cornices above and below windows
- Ornamentation—used lightly at first—later overdone

BAROQUE 1600 to 1760 A.D. *St. Peters Basilica, Vatican; Palazzo Valmarano, Vicenza; The Louvre, Paris; Palace at Versailles.*

- Fundamental forms overflow into each other
- New harmony between forms
- Painting promoted perspective effects
- Architecture, painting, sculpture interacted in harmony
- Michelangelo Buonarotti, Lorenzo Bernini, Claude Perrault, Johann Arnold Nering prominent architects

ROCOCO 1700 to 1750 A.D. *Sans Souci, Potsdam, Altenburg monastery, Vienna.*

- Last period of Baroque, originated in France
- Light-hearted style
- Rococo might be called Baroque on a reduced scale
- Oval floor plans and curved lines
- Ornamentation achieved through detailed stucco work.

NEO-CLASSIC 1800 to 1850 A.D. *St. Paul's Cathedral, London; The Queen's House at Greenwich; Altes Museum, Berlin.*

- Reacted against showy, pretentious style of Baroque
- Return to the Classical style—Doric, Ionic, or Corinthian columns used
- Concerned itself with the problems of everyday life
- Archaic classical forms used
- Inigo Jones, Christopher Wren, and Karl Friedrich Schinkel prominent architects

HISTORICISM 1850 to 1900 A.D. *Eiffel Tower, Paris*

- No significant architectural style
- Many previous styles used simultaneously
- Egyptian, Byzantine, Romanesque, and Gothic
- Technical trickeries possible using new materials such as cast iron
- Alexandre Gustav Eiffel notable architect

ART NOUVEAU 1890 to 1905 A.D. *Church of Sagrada Familia, Park Guell, Barcelona, Spain.*

- Protest against previous styles
- Plant-like curves
- Hyperbolas, parabolas
- Curves running into infinity
- Antonio Gaudi, August Endell, Viktor Horta prominent architects

NEW REALISM 1905 to . . . *Bauhaus Studios and Workshops, Dessau; AEG turbine factory, Berlin; Weissenhof Settlement, Stuttgart; Notre Dame du Haut, Ronchamp, Alsace.*

- Style emphasizes good form and logical planning
- Building's function, proportion, and appearance important
- Cubical and rectangular forms
- Hyperbola and parabola in harmony with geometric forms
- Walter Gropius, Peter Behrens, Le Corbusier, Henri van de Velde prominent architects

MODERN 1905 to . . . *Stazione Termini, Palazzetto dello Sport, Rome, Johnson Wax Factory, Wisconsin, Marina City, Chicago, TWA Terminal , New York, National Gymnasium, Tokyo, The Congress Building, Brasilia.*

- Not yet a title for the present style
- Technology plays a key role
- Prefabricated materials
- Support of buildings has moved from external walls to interior
- Energy conservation, economics important
- Efficient use of space is necessary
- Ludwig Mies van der Rohe, Richard Neutra, Eero Saarinen, Frank Lloyd Wright, Phillip Johnson, and Oscar Niemeyer among leading architects

THE FUTURE Facing all of us in the future are some very difficult problems. Their solutions may lie in new technology or totally unexpected areas. But architects must remain flexible and willing to remember the lessons of the past and to learn the new approaches needed for the future.

NEEDS

- As the architect develops a design, he or she has three areas of need to consider: the needs of the people who will be using the building, the structural needs of the building itself, and the context in which the building is placed. These three areas will almost inevitably conflict with each other; the architect will have to make compromises to come to acceptable solutions.

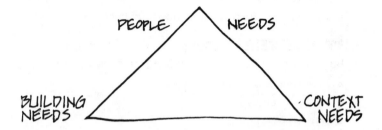

DYNAMIC ALWAYS CHANGING

- Further complicating things is the fact that needs are dynamic, constantly changing. The people who will be using the building will change, and their purposes for using the building will also change. As time passes the environment surrounding the building will change—and often much of the change will occur while the architect is still working on plans.

- The dynamic nature of architecture and need-fulfillment must always be kept in mind and planned for. And when the architect lets one element of need dominate, he or she should do so by conscious choice, knowing that that domination is at the expense of other needs of the architecture.

PEOPLE

- In the end, a building is only an extension of the skin. It is like another set of clothes, extending our controlled environment.

- The architect must consider the basic needs that the design will fulfill.

PHYSIOLOGICAL Must maintain balance, providing adequate air, livable temperature, waste disposal, water.

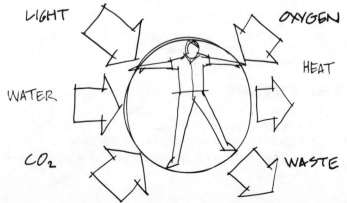

- Must fit human scale, being sized to a person and not to an ant or an elephant.

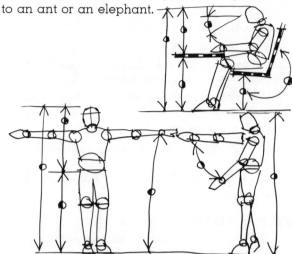

- Must be adequate in terms of the senses, being designed for comfort in terms of noise, light, temperature, humidity, ventilation.

PSYCHOLOGICAL Must provide a sense of safety and security; must allow sufficient space and privacy.

- Must support ego and sense of self-esteem—in the end, a person's image of himself will be dictated, at least in part, by his image of the building he lives or works in.

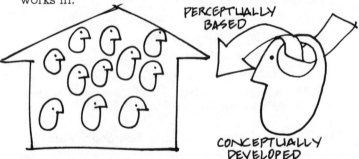

SOCIOLOGICAL Must reflect the fact that most of our needs are met through others.

- Must provide for interaction with others, allowing for public space as well as private.

BUILDING

- Different elements must be considered in dealing with the needs of the building itself:

PROTECTION Must protect both the occupants and the contents of the building.

- Must resist extremes, such as fire or earthquake.

- Must protect against the weather, including such forces as water, cold, heat, and so forth.

IS IT STRUCTURALLY SOUND?

WEIGHT Must be able to stand up under its own weight, plus that of its contents.

HOMEOSTASIS - BALANCE

COMFORT Must maintain a stable and comfortable living and working environment—for instance, appropriate lighting, good air temperature, comfortable humidity, and adequate circulation.

A BUILDING IS A CONTAINER FOR PEOPLE AND THINGS PEOPLE USE.

FLOW Must allow convenient entrance and exit of both materials and people.

DISTRIBUTION Must have proper internal arrangements for distribution of energy, information, and various materials.

CONTEXT

■ The context of the building fits into these categories:

CULTURE Includes the dominant culture of the area, along with its historical, religious, and political elements.

ALWAYS LINKED

NEVER IN ISOLATION

ENVIRONMENT A building cannot be isolated from its surroundings—if it doesn't work with them, it will work against them.

CONNECTIONS Must be connected with outside channels, such as electric power sources, telephone lines, sewer systems, transportation systems.

ECONOMIC Must be economically feasible to build and maintain.

FLEXIBLE Must be designed to change with changing needs.

MEANS

■ The three elements of need in architecture—people, building, and context—can be met in a variety of ways.

PEOPLE'S NEEDS Consider the points of view of different potential users of the building. What will this one need to use the building for? What is his or her attitude toward the structure? Point of view will vary according to the user and the user's needs. Consider how these people will view the building:

- Office workers
- Cleaning people
- Maintenance workers
- Visitors
- Salesmen
- Delivery people
- Meter readers
- Security workers
- Building supervisors
- Consultants

BUILDING NEEDS To meet the needs of the building itself, review similar situations. Learn from the successes and failures of others. A group of Florida architects designed a shopping mall for a Utah city. They failed to consider all the needs of the building, failed to consider the weight that snow would put on the roof. The result: a roof that collapsed.

CONTEXT NEEDS When considering context, analyze the details of the building's environment. Then project into the future to determine how that environment will change in the years to come. An educated guess will still only be a guess—but if it's *educated* it will give you some useful information to determine the needs of the context of the building you're designing.

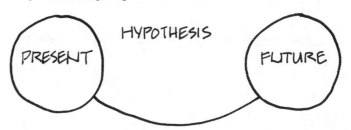

HYPOTHESIS

PRESENT   FUTURE

MECHANISMS

BUILDING
AN EXTENSION OF SELF

A building is like a person. In fact, people have created structures as extensions of themselves, because their own bodies were an inadequate defense against the elements.

■ A person has skin. The building has an outside covering.

■ A person has a heart to circulate blood through the body. The building has heating and ventilation.

■ A person has nerves to control the functions of the different parts of the body. The building has electrical wiring.

■ A person has digestion and waste disposal systems. And so does a building, with its plumbing and sewage systems.

■ A person has personality. So does a building.

■ Both the body and the building are primarily concerned with the maintenance of equilibrium—of balance.

■ Both are concerned with protection from outside forces—from outside extremes.

■ Both are affected by outside factors—wind, temperature, sun, rain, orientation, exposure, surfaces, openings, etc.

SYSTEMS TO MAINTAIN
BALANCE

■ Both people and buildings are organized *systems*, that work in unity to maintain balance and protection from extremes. The following pages explain the mechanisms that maintain a building's balance.

8

MECHANISMS

HEATING The heating system is vital. It controls:

- the temperature of the air;
- the temperature of the surfaces in the building;
- the humidity in the air;
- the circulation of the air;
- the odors in the air;
- the amount of dust in the air;
- the mental state and comfort of those in the building.

■ Heating is controlled by one of several systems: radiant heat, warm air, steam heat, heat pump, hot water heat, combustion or solar heating.

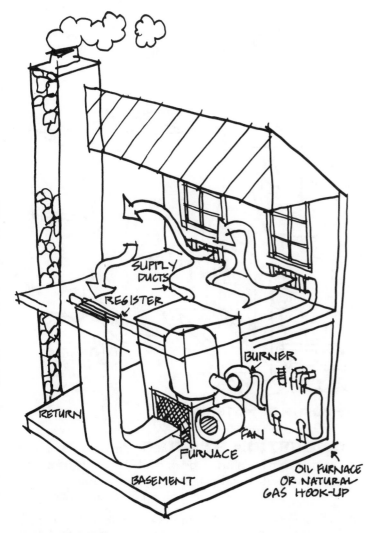

WARM AIR This system controls the temperature at the same time as it controls the volume of air in the room. Air is constantly being redistributed through the building—without drafts. Generally the air is heated at a central location before it's distributed throughout the building.

■ Warm air systems circulate the air better than other systems. They avoid layering of heat and cold. Fresh air can be added to the system, and controls for humidity, ventilation, and air conditioning can be incorporated.

■ These systems have drawbacks, however: they circulate dust and pollen, the duct-work is bulky, and they are not as quiet as water or radiant systems.

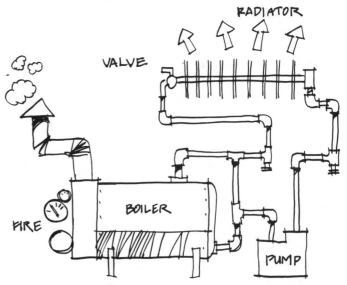

STEAM HEAT This kind of heat is produced in a boiler. The steam is then pumped through pressured and insulated pipes. When the steam reaches its destination, the radiator, the steam is condensed and the heat is released into the room through convection. The condensed water is then pumped back to the boiler through return pipes.

■ With steam heat, it's difficult to have precise temperature control.

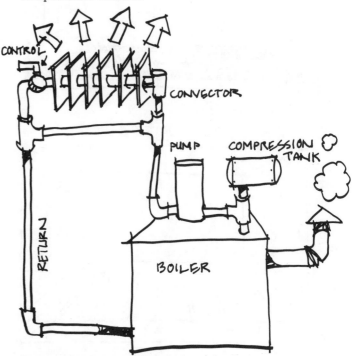

HOT WATER HEAT This type of system circulates heated water through pipes. Heat is controlled by regulating the temperature of the water and its rate of circulation.

MECHANISMS

■ The system is silent and gives good control of heat. Corrosion, however, is often a problem.

■ Hot water heat can also be found in a small, self-contained system. Such systems are usually installed in rooms as baseboard heaters.

RADIANT HEAT Radiant heat comes from hot water or from an electrical system. In the hot water type, water is heated by a boiler, then is carried by pipes to surfaces called panels. The hot water flows through parallel rows of tubes in the panels.

■ In the electrical system, electricity is carried to panels of small wires which the electricity heats.

■ Radiant heat gives an invisible heat source. It generally provides a lower room air-temperature than other systems. It also has a slow-reacting time, and it requires more insulation than other kinds of heating.

■ Electric heat is relatively expensive.

HEAT LOSS

VENTILATION MANDATORY

COMBUSTIBLE MATERIAL

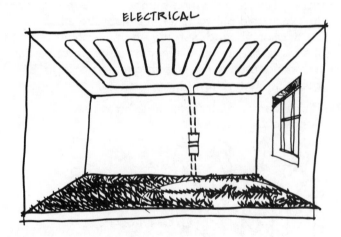

ELECTRICAL

HOT WATER

COMBUSTION HEATING This source of heat comes from burning wood or coal. It is really a form of radiant heat. Combustion heating is probably the most psychologically nourishing of all the systems.

■ Those who use combustion heating generally have two choices:

1. **The fireplace.** This is very inefficient. Warm air escapes up the chimney.

2. **The enclosed stove.** This can be quite efficient, particularly if it uses an outside air source. If it's improperly installed, however, it may cause asphyxiation in an airtight room.

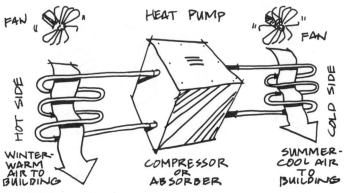

HEAT PUMP Heat pumps extract the heat from the outside air and "pump" it indoors. In the summer, the cycle is reversed: the heat is pumped outdoors. The same unit, therefore, performs both heating and air conditioning functions. The pump automatically heats or cools, depending on the unit setting and the room temperature.

■ A heat pump is composed of three basic elements: an outdoor coil, an indoor coil, and a compressor.

■ Insulation is critical to the heat pump's effectiveness. In extreme cold climate, the building may need a supplementary heat source.

SOLAR SYSTEMS Solar systems have many benefits: they're relatively cost-free to operate, they're nonpolluting, the source of heat is automatically renewable.

■ They have drawbacks, though. They're limited by the orientation of the sun, by the climate, and by the surroundings (trees, geographical features, other buildings). At the present state-of-the-art, solar systems are generally usable for only part of a building's heat.

■ Solar heating is available in both active and passive heating systems.

ACTIVE SOLAR SYSTEMS These systems pump either water or air through the system. A collector panel traps and stores the heat—the water or air help to store it. Generally a large storage container of liquid rods or salts is used.

■ The active solar system is expensive to install. It requires mechanical equipment with electrical power. The system is much more complicated than a passive system, but its heat production is usually better.

PASSIVE SOLAR SYSTEMS Passive systems use a combination of insulation, circulation, and heat collection through windows. To be completely effective, the windows must be oriented for maximum winter sunlight and minimum summer sunlight. Even then, there is often a problem of overheating the house during summer days.

■ These systems also have a problem with heat storage—if the climate has a significant sequence of cold days and cold nights, auxiliary heating is usually required.

■ Heavy insulation of the building includes insulating the glass at night with shutters or heavy curtains to resist the high heat-loss through the windows.

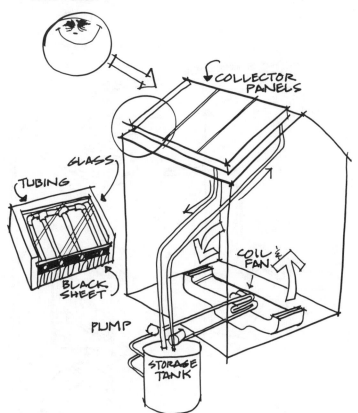

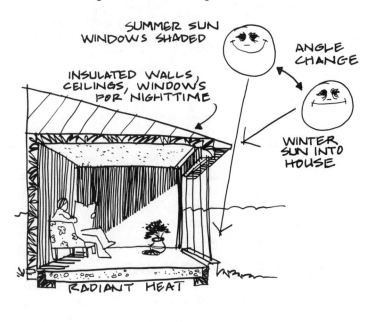

MECHANISMS

AIR COOLING Air cooling can provide a much more comfortable working and living environment. Coupled with a heating system, it can allow the inhabitants of the building to enjoy a constant temperature year-round.

■ There are basically two kinds of air cooling systems: central and evaporative. Both are based on these concepts:

1. As air expands and evaporates, it absorbs heat;

2. As air compresses and absorbs more moisture, it releases heat.

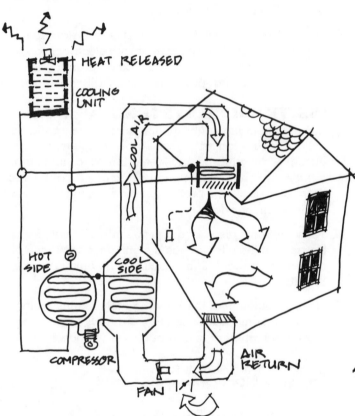

CENTRAL AIR CONDITIONING This kind of cooling is compatible with a forced warm-air system. It cools an entire house, but is expensive to install. Smaller units are available; these are installed in a window. They operate on the same principle as the larger units, but are only effective in cooling a single room or set of rooms.

EVAPORATIVE COOLERS These coolers are cheap to operate—the basic cost is electricty to run the fan. Evaporative coolers effectively move large volumes of air through a building. They are best in areas that have a low level of humidity.

AIR VENTILATION Ventilation systems work on the basic principle that hot air rises and cold air descends. They also recognize that air moves from areas of high pressure to areas of low pressure.

■ Ventilation needs clean outside air to function properly. Since the system neither heats nor cools, this air should be of the right temperature. The system is also at the mercy of the outside air movement. Not enough wind or breeze restricts ventilation; too much gives too much air flow.

■ A window or vent opening is commonly used to ventilate the air. A screen is needed to keep out bugs and birds. Mechanical assistance, such as a fan, is often needed to assist the system. Tightly fitted buildings work the least effectively on this kind on system—they're the best for heating, however.

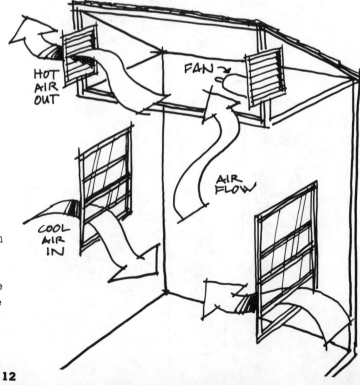

MECHANISMS

WATER SYSTEMS All living systems take in and use water. A building, as an extension of human living systems, must also take in and use water. Freshness is essential. People have historically located where they could be near good sources of fresh water.

■ Water needs to be pressurized to flow through the system. The pipes are arranged to utilize either gravity or pumps—or a combination of the two.

■ To be utilized by people, the water must also have its impurities removed or treated.

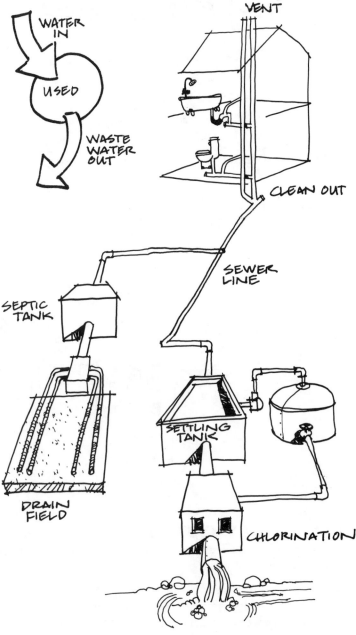

WATER IN

USED

WASTE WATER OUT

VENT

CLEAN OUT

SEWER LINE

SEPTIC TANK

SETTLING TANK

DRAIN FIELD

CHLORINATION

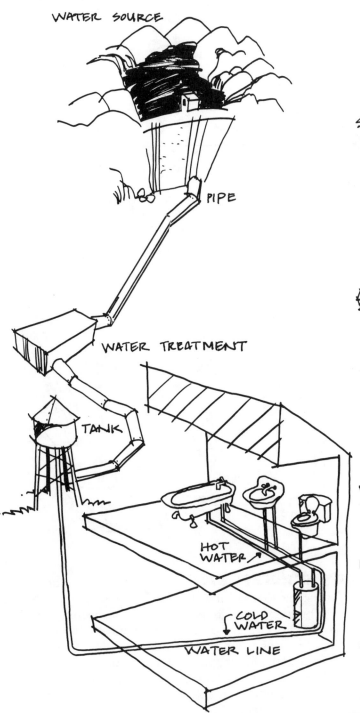

WATER SOURCE

PIPE

WATER TREATMENT

TANK

HOT WATER

COLD WATER

WATER LINE

WASTE SYSTEMS All living systems produce waste. The building must be constructed to accommodate our wastes. If the wastes are not removed, disease and death will usually be the result.

■ There are two common methods of waste disposal:

1. Septic tank. This is a small independent unit that stores the waste underground. Each building usually has its own tank.

2. Sewage system. This interconnects many waste systems. The waste is moved through pipes to a central treatment plant. Entire cities may be connected through the same overall sewage system.

MECHANISMS

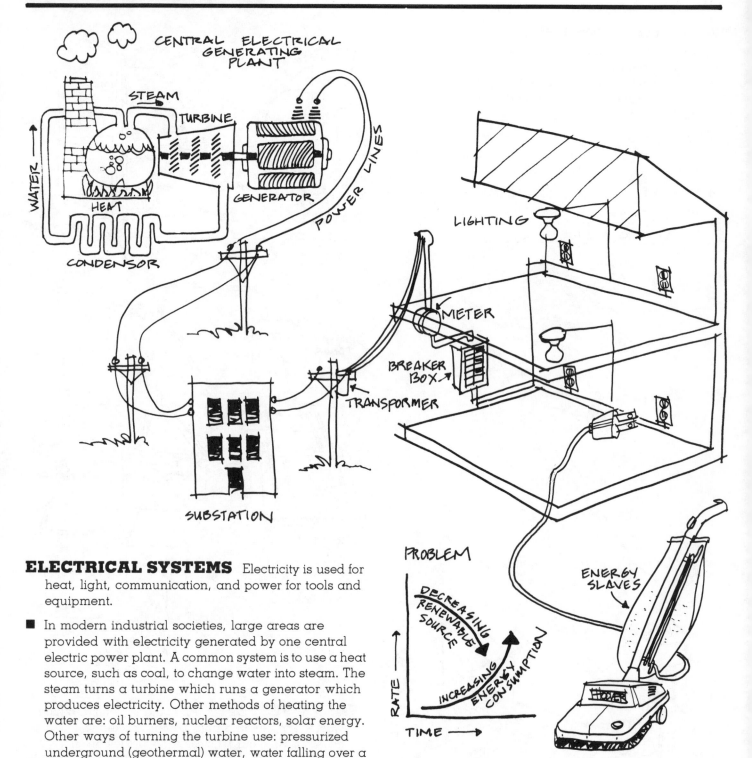

CENTRAL ELECTRICAL GENERATING PLANT

STEAM

TURBINE

GENERATOR

WATER

HEAT

CONDENSOR

POWER LINES

SUBSTATION

TRANSFORMER

LIGHTING

METER

BREAKER BOX

PROBLEM

DECREASING RENEWABLE SOURCE

INCREASING ENERGY CONSUMPTION

RATE

TIME

ENERGY SLAVES

ELECTRICAL SYSTEMS
Electricity is used for heat, light, communication, and power for tools and equipment.

- In modern industrial societies, large areas are provided with electricity generated by one central electric power plant. A common system is to use a heat source, such as coal, to change water into steam. The steam turns a turbine which runs a generator which produces electricity. Other methods of heating the water are: oil burners, nuclear reactors, solar energy. Other ways of turning the turbine use: pressurized underground (geothermal) water, water falling over a dam, wind, tides.

- The energy produced at these central locations is of extremely high voltage. This high voltage is reduced for home and business use, first by substations and then by transformers.

- Electricity is a vital need of our technological society. Our consumption is fast approaching the maximum sustainable levels of power power production. How will we get additional electricity in the future? Will we find other ways to generate it? Or will we be forced to lower our consumption?

OTHER SYSTEMS
A building needs many other systems to make it work. For example, crucial parts of a building include its fire protection, security, and communication systems. The architect must carefully consider the building as a whole entity, then design each of the individual systems as parts of that whole. If the architect has done his or her work well, the finished product will be an entity as workable and unified as a human body.

14

STRUCTURAL CONCEPTS

■ The architect borrows freely from structural engineering, making certain that the building's design provides adequate strength and stability. All materials and their design are based on the structural engineering principles shown on this page.

■ In creating the ideal design, the architect works closely with engineers and builders. A building is constantly being pushed and pulled by a variety of forces: gravity, the weight of the people who use it, the weight of the equipment, winds, and so forth. Its design must be carefully planned to withstand these forces.

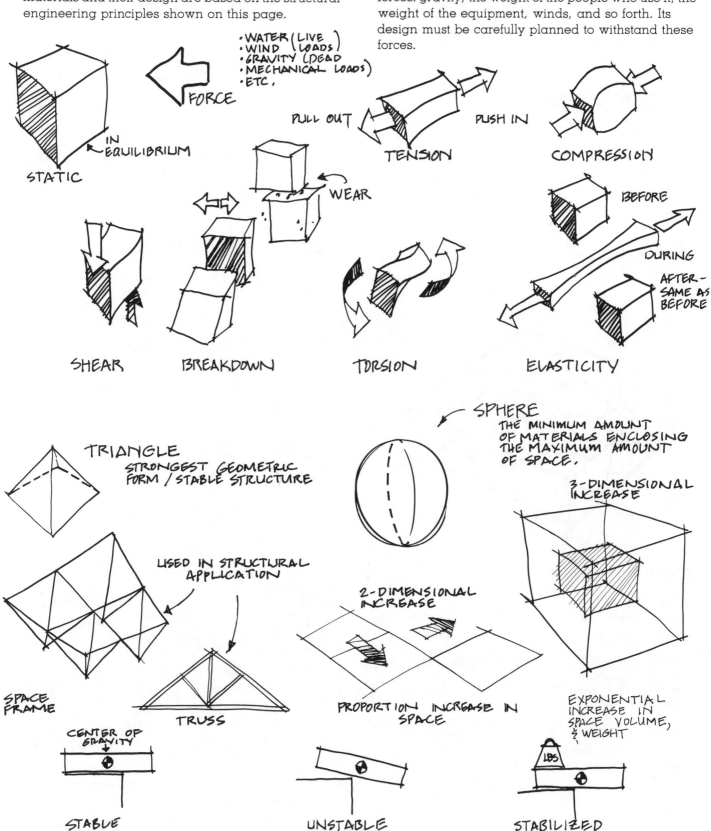

STATIC — IN EQUILIBRIUM

FORCE — •WATER (LIVE) •WIND (LOADS) •GRAVITY (DEAD •MECHANICAL LOADS) •ETC.

TENSION — PULL OUT

COMPRESSION — PUSH IN

WEAR

SHEAR

BREAKDOWN

TORSION

ELASTICITY — BEFORE / DURING / AFTER — SAME AS BEFORE

TRIANGLE — STRONGEST GEOMETRIC FORM / STABLE STRUCTURE

USED IN STRUCTURAL APPLICATION

SPACE FRAME

TRUSS

SPHERE — THE MINIMUM AMOUNT OF MATERIALS ENCLOSING THE MAXIMUM AMOUNT OF SPACE.

2-DIMENSIONAL INCREASE

3-DIMENSIONAL INCREASE

PROPORTION INCREASE IN SPACE

EXPONENTIAL INCREASE IN SPACE VOLUME, & WEIGHT

CENTER OF GRAVITY — STABLE

UNSTABLE

LBS — STABILIZED

15

STRUCTURAL SYSTEMS

■ The architect had a wide number of options to choose from when designing structural systems. Each kind of system performs a different function; each fits in a different kind of situation. At least some of this variety of systems should be considered as possible options when creating a building solution. Here are the most common structural systems architects use.

HOWE

BOWSTRING

FLAT HOWE

SYSTEM TYPES

- Space frame
- Flat truss
- Geodesic dome
- Pneumatic
- Slabs
- Rigid frames
- Tensile
- Vaults
- Folded plates
- Tension cables
- Domes
- Beams
- Arch
- Shells

FLAT TRUSS SYSTEMS

- Two dimensional system
- Constructed with wood, steel, concrete
- Top and bottom cord separated by triangular web members
- Effective in long span structures requiring uninterrupted floor space
- Efficient in making most use of least weight
- Loads are distributed effectively by triangular members
- Trusses are used in series with cross bracing to stabilize structure against lateral loads
- Different type trusses can be mixed
- Basic trusses are: King Post, Queen Post, Town or Lattice, Warren, Bowstring, Pratt, Flat Pratt, Howe, Flat Howe, Fink, Fan Fink, Scissors

SPACE FRAME

- Three dimensional truss-like assembly
- Rigidly connected short, thin, members
- Based upon forms of triangular geometry, i.e. tetrahedral, octahedral, hexagonal etc.
- Economical for long spans and great spaces
- Requires less material than two-dimensional trusses
- Built of simple prefabricated members
- Delicate, lightweight frames
- Supporting columns and wall structure require bracing against lateral loads
- Connecting joints require care in design and construction
- Konrad Wachsmann is a pioneer in space frame research and design

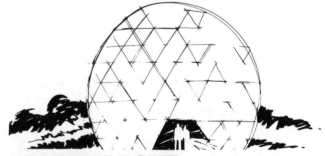

GEODESIC DOME

- Curved truss system
- Triangulated lattice work
- Short, thin, rigid members
- Light but stable structure
- Design and construction of connecting joints is a crucial point
- Encloses enormous areas without internal support
- Walls and roof are single unit
- Dome cannot be penetrated for openings such as doors or windows without structural weakening
- Interior structures must be independant of dome
- Invented by R. Buckminister Fuller

STRUCTURAL SYSTEMS

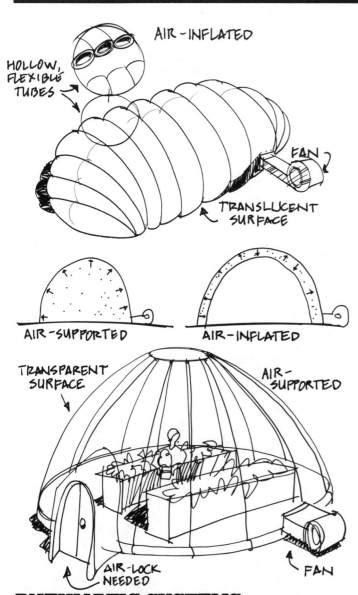

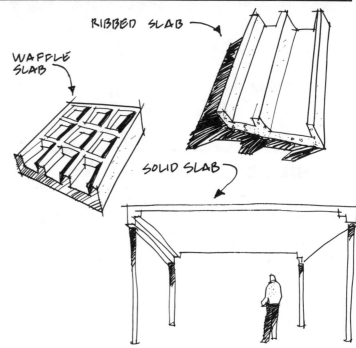

SLAB SYSTEM

- Broad, shallow, reinforced concrete beam
- Transmits loads laterally to supports at ends in the same way as a beam
- One-way slab spans two parallel beams or walls
- Ribbed slab is a one-way slab system with much of the concrete left out of between reinforcing rods on bottom to save weight in longer spans

- Two-way slab spans between columns in a square pattern
- Waffle slab is a two-way slab system with much of the concrete left out between reinforcing rods on bottom to save weight in longer spans
- Slabs have limited spans but are simple and used widely

PNEUMATIC SYSTEMS

- Sometimes referred to as *fluid-filled structures*
- Air is fluid most commonly used
- Two types—Air-inflated or Air-supported
- Air-inflated: made of fabric tubes or lenses braced by internal air pressure
- Air-inflated: capable of relatively short spans
- Air-supported: theoretically capable of unlimited spans
- Air-supported: fabric directly supported by air pressure against its inside surface

- Lightweight flexible, airtight membranes: plastic, vinyl, teflon coated fiberglass
- Enclosure supported by slight difference in air pressure between inside and outside
- Continuous air pressure source needed
- Large enclosures at relatively low cost
- Entrance through an air lock door
- Unstable in winds
- Many applications, transportable, temporary coverings
- Originally U.S. Air Force radar installation coverings

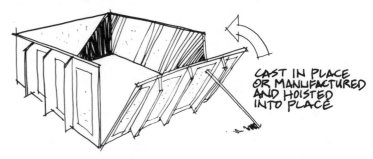

FRAME SYSTEM

- Rigid frame structure
- Joins beam and supporting columns with rigid connection
- Fabricated in one piece
- Reduces bending stress in beam
- Allows greater spans with less material

- Made generally of rolled steel, or pre-cast concrete
- Reduced size of members compared with conventional beam and column systems
- Dead weight less—allowing greater spans

STRUCTURAL SYSTEMS

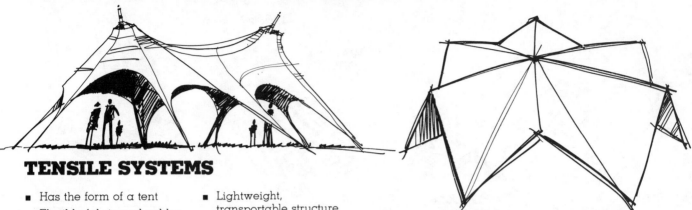

TENSILE SYSTEMS

- Has the form of a tent
- Flexible fabric and cables stretched over vertical posts and anchored to ground
- Posts create high points that tension the fabric and cables
- Large spaces can be covered
- Lightweight, transportable structure
- *Flutter* due to wind pressures is problem
- *Flutter* controlled by keeping loose edges of fabric taut
- Separate structure generally needed to enclose sides from weather

FOLDED PLATE SYSTEMS

- Bent surfaces generally made of thin concrete and steel reinforcing mesh
- Bending creates rigidity and strength
- Longer spans achieved with less material
- Strength gained through geometry of the folds
- Forming and shoring is often difficult and expensive with complex folded surfaces

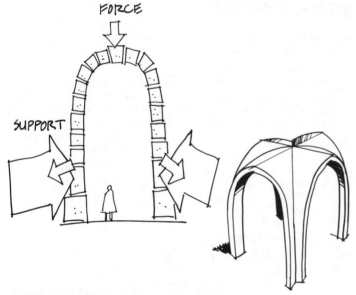

VAULTED SYSTEMS

- Masonry blocks fitted together to form an elongated arch
- Tunnel vault is simplest
- Works on principle of compression much as arch and dome do
- Enormous compressive and frictional forces created between blocks
- Keystones running along the spine of vault are critical to stablizing the compression and friction needed to bind vault together
- Vaulted cathedrals required another roof over vault to protect it from weather
- Wall buttressing (or flying buttresses) required to keep vault from collapse
- Impractical today because of high weight-to-span ratio and massive masonry effort involved

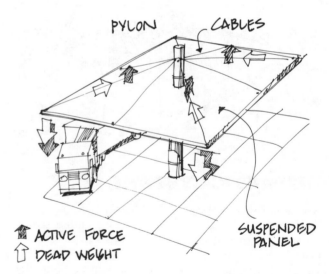

CABLE SYSTEM

- Non-rigid flexible cable secured by fixed ends
- Cable supports itself
- Cable spans space by transferring external loads normal to curve through simple tensile stresses
- Low weight-to-span ratio allows economy in spanning great distances
- Low weight-to-span ratio makes cable susceptible to *flutter* as a result of wind uplift.
- *Flutter* remedied by increasing dead weight on cable or by using tie downs from cable to ground

STRUCTURAL SYSTEMS

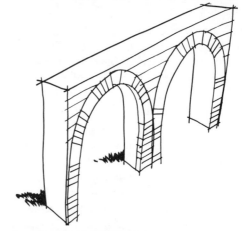

DOME SYSTEMS

- Dome is an arch rotated about a circular plan
- Works on principle of compression like arch and vault
- Compression ring like keystone of arch is critical element in stablizing the compression and friction needed to bind it together
- Requires heavy masonry
- Requires enormous footings and thick drums to sit on
- Ancients could span great space with domes

ARCH SYSTEMS

- Stone blocks cut and fitted to form curved shape
- Must be anchored firmly at each end to transmit loads to supports
- Keystone critical to stablize compression and friction needed to bind arch together
- Aesthetically very graceful
- Creats larger, more open spaces
- Requires massive foundations and massive masonry effort
- Susceptible to additional stresses caused by expansion and contraction
- Developed by early Romans

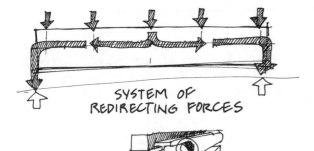

SYSTEM OF REDIRECTING FORCES

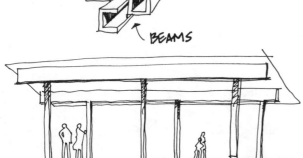

BEAMS

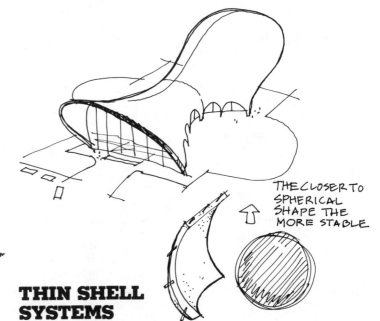

THE CLOSER TO SPHERICAL SHAPE THE MORE STABLE

BEAM SYSTEM

- Solid, generally straight, structural elements
- Made of reinforced concrete, wood (solid or laminated), or rolled steel sections
- Develops compressive and tensile stresses
- Transmits loads laterally along axis to supports at ends
- Simple system with limited spans due to heavy weight-to-span ratio
- Works best in short span applications
- Greater spans possible with new technological developments with materials

THIN SHELL SYSTEMS

- Thin self-supporting membrane usually of concrete over steel reinforcing mesh
- Works on eggshell principle
- More definition in the curvature of the shell makes a more stable structure
- Efficient for long span structures
- Can be free form and aesthetically very exciting
- Enormous lateral thrust at base of shell must be counteracted to prevent collapse

MATERIALS

- The architect must understand the complex topic of materials and the relationship between those materials, architecture, and technology. There are many building materials available; there are also many questions to ask about those materials.

  - How does the material react under stress?
  - What does the material look like?
  - What is the color or colors of the material?
  - Are different materials compatible with each other?
  - How expensive are the materials?
  - Are they easy or difficult for a builder to work with?
  - Are they readily available in the necessary amounts?
  - How does technology make possible material uses in new and exciting ways?
  - Which materials lend themselves to things like solar heating?

- Building materials, are discussed in more detail on the following pages. They are divided into five basic categories: Rock, Organic, Metal, Synthetic, and Hybrid.

ROCK

- Natural material like stone or clay that is used in much the same form as it is found in natural deposits.

ASBESTOS Best known for its nonflammability. It is also resistant to heat, moisture, corrosion, and a number of chemicals.

FORMS
- Asbestos-cement board and sheet

- Asbestos-cement corrugated sheet

- Asbestos-cement piping

- Asbestos paper

USES
- Walls, ceilings, soffits, partitions, dividers, roofs. Resists alkali, acid, rot, mold, fungus, insects, rodents.

- Roofs, and siding. Corrugations enhance strength. Resists acid fumes, corrosive smoke, decay, rust, weather extremes, termites.

- Large and small, pressure and non-pressure—water, sewer, storm drain, and industrial process pipes. Resists rust, rot, rodents, termites, sewer, soil corrosion.

- Fire retardant in roofing felts, light fixtures, heat convectors, cooking and heating appliances, with wood and metal for fire-proof doors and partitions.

ASPHALT A brown to black bituminous hydrocarbon found naturally or manufactured as a by-product in petroleum refining. It is water-proof, adhesive, and resistant to most acids and alkalis. Its greatest strength is its binding ability.

FORMS
- Asphalt coating

- Asphalt paving

- Asphalt resilient flooring

- Asphalt roofing and siding

USES
- Waterproofing concrete or masonry below grade.

- Paving for streets, parking areas, driveways, airport runways, sidewalks, playgrounds, etc.

- Fire-resistant, colorful, flooring material, cove bases, and trim strips.

- Saturating felt to underlay shingles and siding, a base ingredient for roofing cements, an ingredient in shingles (roll, strip, and single units).

BRICK Small, common building unit, rectangular in shape, is composed of inorganic substances that are hardened by heat or chemicals. Can be divided into two categories: **1.** Hard burned and soft burned, (clay fired to hardness) **2.** Cement brick and sand-lime brick, made of cementitious materials hardened by chemical process.

FORMS
- Burned brick

- Cement brick

- Sand-lime brick

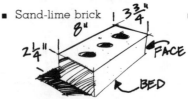

USES
- Common building brick, facing brick, glazed facing brick, fire brick, acid brick, sewer brick.

- Veneer and facing for exterior walls where high strength and moisture resistance are needed.

- Common building brick and other applications similar to burned brick. Has good frost, fire, and acid resistance.

CLAY There are several different kinds of clays, which differ in composition and potential use. Clay is valuable in commercial ceramics because it is flexible when wet and hardens when heated. Most clays come from aluminous or silicate rocks.

FORMS
- Clay tile veneer

USES
- Ornamentation on masonry, walls, or external plaster. Can be colored, plain, decorated, or textured. Physical characteristics similar to those of burned brick.

- Clay tile pipes and fittings

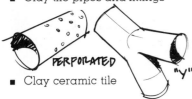

- Clay ceramic tile

- Clay tile flue linings

- Clay tile roofing

- Structural clay tile

- Foundation drains, subsoil sewage drains, subsoil gutters, drainage for athletic fields, highways, and recreation areas.

- Floor and wall tile in these forms; glazed wall tile, quarry tile, mosaic tile. and paver tile, various moldings, caps, corners, and angle pieces.

- Protection for masonry around flue, and to prevent build-up of soot in chimneys.

- Permanent, fire-proof, strong structure, variety of textures and colors available.

- Non-load-bearing tile is used for interior walls, to protect steel structural beams, girders, and columns from fire. Load-bearing tile is used for exposed or faced load bearing walls.

PERLITE A glass-like, volcanic rock. Expands into a light, fluffy substance when heated.

FORMS
- Insulation

- Fire-proofing

- Additive

USES
- Acoustic and thermal insulator when combined with concrete, plaster, or stucco. Also lightweight insulation in loose-fill applications.

- Fire-proofing when combined with plaster, stucco, or concrete.

- Filler for paints, plaster, roofing tile, fire brick, and filter material.

SAND: Artificially or naturally disintegrated rock and/or minerals from many different sources.

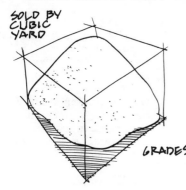

USES
- Construction and paving. Important element in the mixing of stucco, mortar, cement, etc.

STONE A number of kinds of stone are used in construction.

FORMS
- Granite

- Limestone

- Marble

- Slate

USES
- Igneous rock used as veneer in sawed or polished form. Cut to form sills, copings, columns, stair treads, lintels, door and window trims. Flagstones used for paving, walls, and curbing. Broken and used for highway fills, railroad ballast and crushed for use in terrazzo and artificial stone.

- Sedimentary rock used for veneer, sills, door trims, wall construction, concrete, paving fill, and surface finish.

- Polished limestone used for interior and exterior floor and veneer applications. Durable in dry atmosphere. Crushed limestone used as aggregate in terrazzo, artificial stone and as finish for built-up roofs.

- Metamorphic rock used as roofing, flooring, interior and exterior facings and sills, blackboards, and countertops.

ORGANIC

- Wood and similar materials composed of cells. Called organic because they come from living *organisms*—plants.

CORK The spongy bark of an oak tree grown in Europe and in Africa. Has a number of properties that make it valuable. It is buoyant, elastic, and resistant to both air and water.

FORMS
- Cork sheet and board

- Cork block

- Ground cork

USES
- Bulletin boards, acoustic insulation, vibration reduction, and thermal insulation.

- Heat and acoustic insulation in refrigeration piping, ducts, etc.

- Additive in resilient flooring, and fire brick.

MATERIALS

PAPER Made from the wood fibers of trees, mechanically processed with chemicals and formed into various products.

FORMS

- Paper products

- Paper pulp decking

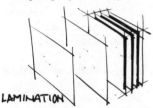

LAMINATION

- Paper pulp sheets

USES

- Roofing felts, building paper, flashing, insulation, protective coatings, bags, wrappers, boxes, concrete form preparation, etc.
- Vapor barriers, nailing surfaces, thermal and acoustic insulation by laminating and/or impregnating it with—asbestos cement, metal foil, plastic film, waterproof adhesives, asphalt, etc.
- Surface finish of interior walls and ceilings, as core material, in corrugated or cellular form for doors, partitions, and furniture.

WOOD: Divided into two categories—hardwood (from deciduous trees that shed leaves at the end of each summer) and soft wood (from evergreens that don't shed needles or scales seasonally). Wood is a highly useful building material desired for its strength, light weight, and durablity. It is easily worked and provides many colors, textures, and grain patterns.

FORMS

- Structural

- Unfinished

- Exterior finish

- Interior finish

- Milled

USES

- Trusses, girders, beams, rafters, posts, studs, sills, plates, decking, and laminated structural members.
- Cross bracing, subflooring, blocking, sheathing, furring, lathing, stair stringers, etc.
- Trim, roofing, siding, railings, gutters, moldings, stairs, board and batten, facias, etc.
- Paneling, stairs, flooring, shelving, decorative moldings, etc.
- Pre-fabricated doors, windows, screens, stairs, railings, cabinets, shutters, mantels, moldings, trims, etc.

METAL

- Natural materials not used in their original state. Aluminum, copper, iron, and others must be refined before they are used. Most metals conduct heat and electricity.

ALUMINUM An easily shaped blueish silver-white metal, it is light, soft, nonmagnetic, has good electrical and thermal conductivity, high reflectivity, and is resistant to oxidation.

FORMS

- Aluminum alloy

- Aluminum foil

- Corrugated aluminum

- Aluminum mesh

- Aluminum sheet

- Aluminum wire

USES

- Combination of aluminum and other metals. Used in railings, panels, supports, insulation, siding, weather stripping, framing, trim, and molding.
- Comes in thin sheets and is used for insulation, as a vapor barrier, and for protective and decorative finishes.
- Insulation against weather, used in roofing and siding.
- Guards, screens, and fencing. Panels are used in flooring, roofing, siding and partitions. Comes in a wide variety of forms and sizes.
- Awnings, air ducts, trim, molding, walls, tile, and doors. Comes in sheets and coils and can be embossed or plain, corrugated or ribbed.
- Alternative to copper wire in electrical applications.

BRASS An alloy of copper and zinc. The color depends on the quantity of zinc present. Not as strong as steel, but corrosion resistant and easy to solder, weld, polish, or braze.

FORMS

- Sheet, bar, strip, rod, tube, powder, special shapes and castings

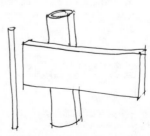

USES

- Used in doors, windows, railings, trim, door and window frames, ornamental metalwork, hardware, hardware plating, ties, weatherstripping, nuts, bolts, screws, anchors. Most brass is used in plumbing and its related areas—heating and air conditioning, and in machinery parts.

BRONZE:
An alloy of copper and tin. Worked by forging, casting, rolling, and extruding.

FORMS
- Statuary bronze

- Hardware bronze

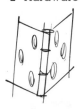

USES
- Casting of statuary, architectural ornamentation and decoration. Color varies with amount of tin included in the alloy.
- Used for rough hardware and accessories, including; weatherstripping, ties for masonry and attaching copper, brass, or bronze, screws, nuts and bolts, washers, anchors, etc.

COPPER
A common reddish metal, ductile and malleable, one of the best conductors of heat and electricity. Easy to work with and strong enough for light structural work. It is resistant to corrosion but not to many common acids.

FORMS
- Copper wire

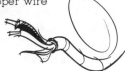

- Copper tubing

- Copper foil

- Copper sheet

USES
- Used for electrical work in the form of wire, cable, bars or rods. In construction it is woven into mesh, for screens, grills, and barriers for protection.
- Used in heating, plumbing, air conditioning, etc.
- Used for flashing, and laminated to other materials for building papers, fabrics, and asphalt compounds.
- Used in roofing in prefabricated shapes for flashing, expansion joints, gravel stop, pipes, etc.

IRON
The most used metal. Easily magnetized. Not resistant to most acids. It is used in the production of steel. Iron is often used in construction.

FORMS
- Cast iron

- Wrought iron

USES
- Easily formed into different shapes, and used for piping, ornamentation, and plumbing fixtures.
- Is one of the most pure forms of iron and is used in piping, plumbing, and heating. Available in pipes, sheets, and bars.

LEAD
A very heavy, workable metal. Good corrosion resistance, relatively high in nuclear radiation resistance.

FORMS
- In extruded form as wire, bends, pipe, rod, ribbon, cames. In rolled form as sheets, foil, strip and blanks. In cast form as die castings, and also other forms—shot, powder, wool, etc.

USES
- Used in paints, caulking, color pigments, hot-dip protective coatings, vibration control, protection against X-rays and gamma rays, coatings for rust resistance for iron and steel, plumbing, electrical cable coverings, etc.

STEEL
Commercial iron alloyed with carbon up to 1.7 percent. Can be wrought, rolled, welded, cast, forged, but not extruded.

FORMS
- Steel reinforcement

REBAR

- Galvanized steel

- Steel mesh

- Steel plate and strip

- Structural steel

- Steel tube

USES
- Comes in bars, mesh, sheet, corrugated, rope. Embedded in concrete to provide extra strength and reinforcement.
- Steel sheet, strip or wire coated with zinc for protection against corrosion. Used for ductwork, roofing, and siding. Galvanized pipe used for items such as culverts and spillways.
- Galvanized or ungalvanized; used as a protection against acid corrosion. Used in fencing and screens. Also used in ornamental ways.
- Used for hollow metalwork and as decking. Also used in doors, windows, and roofing.
- I-beams, H-columns, Z-shapes, T-shapes, angles, channels, plates, in many standard sizes for each type. Used with flexibility in framing, and building up structural members by combining the shapes. Also used in open web joists, trusses and space frame construction.
- Available in many sizes, used for columns, beams, scaffolding, piles, furniture, railings, piping, conduits, etc.

MATERIALS

STAINLESS STEEL
An alloy of steel and chromium. Resistant to heat, rust, and corrosion. May be cast, rolled, drawn, forged, machined, bent, welded, riveted, and formed.

FORMS
- Sheet, strip, tubing, bar, castings, wire, and other forms.

USES
- Flashing, trim, paneling, and doors, grills, screens, countertops, gutters, appliances. Wire is used in the manufacture of nuts and bolts.

TIN
A soft, ductile metal. Usually covered with a thin coat of stannic oxide. Corrosion resistant. Polishes well.

FORMS
- Sheet, foil, wire, tube, pipe, powder, shot, ingot, etc.

USES
- Mirrors, hardware, fusible alloys, solder, bronze and brass alloying, hardware, and for protective coatings on stronger metals, particularly for the food industry.

ZINC
A brittle, hard metal, with low strength characteristics. Resistant to corrosion by water but readily corroded by alkalis and acids. Can be hot- or cold-drawn, extruded, formed, cast, punched, riveted, and welded.

FORMS
- Slab, bar, plate, stick, sheet, wire, tubing, foil, shot, strip, powder, etc.

USES
- Hot-dip galvanizing, die casting metal, alloying ingredient in brass.

SYNTHETIC
- To *synthesize* means to put together; synthetics are materials that are put together, or made, by man. Glass and plastics are both good examples of synthetics.

GLASS
A transparent mixture of silicates, flux and stabilizer fused into a rigid, non-crystalline mass. A versatile construction material.

FORMS
- Glass block
- Foamed glass
- Corrugated glass
- Glass fibers
- Float glass
- Heat strengthened glass

USES
- Insulation, special lighting, or interior panels.
- Insulation.
- Decorative purposes.
- Acoustic work.
- Windows and mirrors.
- Colored panels.

- Insulating glass
- Laminated glass
- Structural glass

- Elimination of glare and heat absorption.
- Bullet-proof windows and safety glasses.
- Bathroom and kitchen partitions and surfaces.

PLASTICS
A group of organic, synthetic, or processed materials that are drawn, molded, extruded, cast, or laminated into filaments, objects, or films. Plastics are being used more and more in modern construction.

FORMS
- Plastics come in a large variety of forms; pipe, fittings, adhesives, fabrics, protective coatings, laminates, caulking and sealing compounds, non-breakable glazing material, water-proofing, thermal insulation, fibers, foams, etc.

USES
- Plastic has a multitude of uses in—pipe fittings, shower stalls, adhesives, tape, cement, flooring, duct insulation, sandwich panels, and electrical insulation, adhesives, refrigerants, artificial leather and fabrics, lacquers, and varnishes, etc.

RUBBER
Obtained from the milky fluid (latex) of *Hevea brasiliensis*, a tropical tree that yields the best natural latex. The synthetic version *polyisoprene* is produced in large volume worldwide and is now more widely used than natural rubber. A unique substance that has many different uses; it retains its elasticity over a wide range of temperatures, serves as an excellent cushion against shock, has a high degree of elasticity and a high degree of resistance to gas and water and lasts for long periods of time.

FORMS
- Extrusions

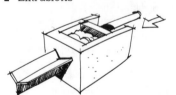

- Flooring

- Adhesives

USES
- Foam or non-foam for filler strips, vibration control materials, closure strips for corrugated sheet materials, expansion joints, glazing, and sealing applications for curtain wall construction,
- Tile and roll floor covering, as pad for carpet, stair treads, protective mats, pads and nosing.
- Mixed with solvents and applied to both surfaces to be adhered, has good moisture resistance and is used generally in interior applications for general purposes.

- Paints and coatings

- Bituminous toppings

- Insulation

- Other

- Water soluble paints and coatings provide washable surfaces with little or no paint odor. Some forms are used in vapor barriers, sealants, water-proof membranes, mortars, and finishes.

- Mixtures of bituminous materials and rubber used for cement toppings, crack and joint fillers, below grade water-proofing, etc.

- Tubular form for residential and industrial plumbing insulation for cold water lines.

- Adhesive tapes, hardware items, washers, belts, wheels, bumpers, etc.

HYBRID

- A hybrid is something of mixed origin; it is made by combining two or more materials together.

CEMENT A powder of silica, alumina, lime, and other minerals used to bring non-adhesive materials together in a cohesive, useful whole.

USES

- A binding ingredient in concrete, mortar, plaster and related materials.

CONCRETE A building material made by mixing cement and a mineral aggregate with sufficient water to cause the cement to set and bind the entire mass together. Easy to work with until it sets—then it is quite hard and strong. Aggregate size distinguishes concrete from other hybrids like mortar and plaster.

FORMS

- Plain, reinforced, prestressed, prefabricated.

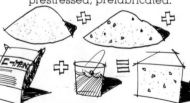

USES

- Pilings, retaining walls, dams, bridges, roads, foundations, structural framing, beams, walls, block, decking, beams, girders, roof and floor tile, pipe, tanks, etc.

MORTAR Like concrete, is a mixture that becomes hard after setting.

USES

- Masonry, tile grouting, plastering, etc.

PLASTER A pasty combination of lime, water, and sand that hardens when dry.

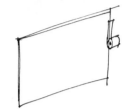

USES

- Coating walls, ceilings, and partitions. Strong, durable. Sometimes used for fire-proofing.

VERMICULITE A thin, mineral construction material.

USES

- Insulation, filling, and fire-proofing.

HARDBOARD Manufactured by compressing shredded wood at high temperatures.

FORMS

- Perforated, prefinished, and smooth. Good resistance to wear, heat, and water.

USES

- Siding, paneling, cabinets, and acoustical material.

PARTICLEBOARD Small wood chips bonded together. Durable. Good finishing and resistance qualities.

USES

- Veneers, cabinets, etc.

PLYWOOD Separate sheets of wood bonded together. One sheet followed by another placed at right angles to the preceding sheet and then bonded. This increases strength.

USES

- Roofing, subflooring, cabinets, and siding. Sometimes covered with plastic, textile, or paper.

- Materials are basically used only in three ways. All of the materials discussed in this section have application only in these three areas:

1. *Structural.* This category includes such things as steel I-beams and two-by-fours, which contribute to the structural integrity of the building.

2. *Systems.* This includes windows for lighting, ducting for heating, insulation for temperature control, and so forth.

3. *Coverings.* Materials are used as coverings in the cases of panelling, plasterboard, carpet, and so on.

FORMS

- Materials come in a wide variety of forms. To be able to work effectively with a given design, an architect must have a good understanding of what forms are available. For example, asphalt will be used differently according to the form it comes in, whether in liquid coating, paving, or felt paper.
A few examples of forms:

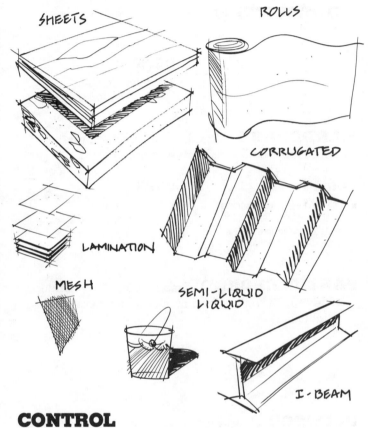

SOURCES

- To be effective, the architect must have a current knowledge of materials, their cost, and their uses, and must also keep informed on the latest architectural ideas and practices. This boils down to having a number of good *sources*.

- **Other architects**—Talk to other architects whose work you respect. Note how they keep up to date. Make a list of sources they find valuable (and those they don't find valuable.)

- **Source catalogues**—which list suppliers, distributors, and manufacturers. Sweet's File is a good example.

- **Thomas Register**—A detailed list of information on manufacturers often containing information that other sources lack. It's available in most libraries.

- **Mailing lists**—Get your name on the mailing list of several suppliers. You'll start getting things regularly.

- **Manufacturer's representatives**—These are essentially salesmen. Get in touch with them and they'll keep you apprised of new developments in materials.

- **Consultants**—The interior designer, the landscape artist, the structural engineer, the mechanical engineer, the lighting expert, and all the others closely follow their own fields and can offer you valuable advice concerning materials.

CONTROL

- Control of materials is essential. Architects who try to use too many *different* materials end up with a hodge-podge. Their costs will soar and their design will lack discipline and consistency. Any design that shows an inconsistency in its final creation reflects an inconsistency in the material chosen, methodology used, and personalities involved.

MULTIPLICITY OF MATERIALS MAY LEAD TO NON-DISCIPLINED AND COSTLY SOLUTIONS

ESTIMATING

- Making estimates is an important part of an architect's job. As an architect, you will need to offer cost estimates for both materials and labor. And, since costs in both areas are constantly changing, you will need to study continually to keep up to date.

- Good source material is vital—you will need to keep informed from books and catalogs that list current information on costs. With such assistance, you'll be able to make accurate estimates as a guide for both the client and the contractor.

- You'll be giving estimates for the following, among others: site work, brick, wood, insulation, doors, windows, finishings, and mechanical and electrical systems. Each of these categories will have many of its own categories. You will also need to know such areas as labor sub-contracting and mark-up.

DESIGN DEVELOPMENT/COMMUNICATION

DEVELOPMENT OF DESIGNS

■ Before you, the architect, can solve a design problem, you've got to be able to *see* the solution, even before it becomes reality. The way you can do that is to visualize all the possible solutions in your head—then quickly transfer those visions onto paper. The key is to get them all down, rapid-fire. The quality of the original sketches doesn't matter. What's important is that you're able to get down as many ideas as possible.

■ Before you proceed too far, you should involve the client as much as possible. Clients often have some definite ideas about what they want and something they say may suggest the very solution you're looking for. If you proceed madly ahead without trying to get such input, you may create something the client absolutely can't live with. Much better to work together from the beginning, so you can find a solution that meets your client's needs as well as the needs of the building.

COMMUNICATION OF THE DESIGN

■ You can have the best design in the world, but it's not going to do you any good unless you're able to communicate it to a client. They need to see how your design is going to meet their needs. And here's the tough part: they need to be able to visualize the building as it will finally be—with them inside it.

■ That's a particularly hard task because you'll be trying to make the presentation in visual terms—and the client may well have a primarily verbal brain. Give your visual presentation, but make sure you accompany it with a good verbal explanation. That will help bridge the gap.

■ Remember that floor plans and schematics don't communicate accurately to most people. You'll want to show those, but only with other tools.

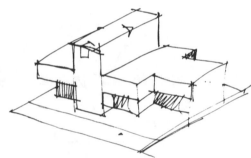

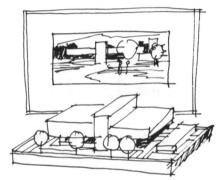

ROUGH SKETCHES These should be the first step in your sketching. Rough is the key word.
Get some cheap and thin tracir g paper to make your series of sketches. Get the kind of writing implement you're comfortable with—a felt pen, a ballpoint, a pencil, chalk—whatever meets your needs. Now, as spontaneously as you can, draw out your ideas as they come to you.

■ Figure that the ideas will come fast and furious. That will tell you how you're going to have to draw.

■ After you've gone through a series and things seem to be slowing down, go back over what you've done. Some of your sketches will stand out as more obvious solutions than the others. Take the ones that work best and use them as models for further development: use the tracing paper to overlay the previous sketches and refine. Gradually you'll evolve a solution that really *works*.

QUICK MODELS After you've gone through the rough sketch process, you can move to another development tool: the quick model.

Take the best sketch you can come up with and turn it into a rough-and-ready model of the building. Rough is the thing to keep in mind. If you try to make it too fancy, it will be hard to change. Just get the idea into some kind of three-dimensional form. Then you can fiddle with it to make it work better.

■ You won't show this quick model to anyone—it's simply a tool to help you evolve the best design you can. Once you have a model you're comfortable with, then you can make a better model. This is called the *presentation model*. Use materials that you can work with easily, such as chipboard or cardboard; hold the thing together with glue.

■ This model stage is essential. Time and again I've thought I had a perfect solution to the design problem—until I tried to make a model of it. Then the problems become glaringly obvious. At the same time, solutions are easier to come up with when you make the switch from flat, one-dimensional drawings to three-dimensional models.

RENDERINGS Renderings are colored, perspective drawings. They'll help give the client a feel for the building from an insider's point of view. They show the building in its complete and final form, with people, furniture, accessories, and so forth. It doesn't matter which media you use for renderings—what's essential is that the renderings be realistic. The client must be able to see himself there. Each completed rendering should be mounted on heavy board before you show it.

PRESENTATION MODELS After the renderings have been approved, you can make a model of the building to show the client. This model can be a further refinement of the quick model you made in the design development stage.

SLIDE PRESENTATIONS Slides are an excellent way to show the client what you have in mind. The slide presentation can include photos of your artwork, as well as examples of other buildings that have successfully resolved the problems you're faced with.

PROCESS/DEVELOPMENT

DESIGN PROCESS The steps outlined here parallel those we covered earlier in the creativity section. No matter how you approach your design, you'll frequently go through the same steps, whether consciously or subconsciously. Those steps will take you all the way through the process, from conception to completion:

IDENTIFY Define what the problem is, making sure you know what needs to be done. Then put down in writing just what kind of building is needed, including the client's needs and financial limitations.

GATHER Bring together all the ideas you can. After you've done a good job of identifying the problem, you can let your mind run free. Whenever you get an idea that might be the solution, or that might lead to the solution, write it down. Some sources of ideas include a review of what others have done in similar situations, brainstorming with others, or simply listing questions you think are important, and then writing the answers. Next, do a series of quick, rough sketches.

REFINE Take the materials and ideas you've gathered and examine each one carefully against the needs you've identified. Reject those that don't meet the criteria; further refine those that *might* fit. Enlarge and refine your sketches.

ANALYZE Consider the work you've done to this point to determine how effective each of your different solutions really is. Create working models of the best.

DECIDE Take a close look at the solutions you're left with and pick the one that works best. If none are satisfactory, return to step 1 and start over again.

IMPLEMENT Now that you've come up with the best possible solution to the design problem, take the steps to make it grow from a small model to a big-as-life reality. This includes getting final approval from the client (including both cost and plans), hiring a contractor, supervising the work, and so on.

FEEDBACK Each design you complete gives you new insights that can be applied to future problems. It's a recurring cycle of design, feedback, design, feedback. Experience is a good teacher, and it's a wise student who can learn from his or her own experience. An even wiser person will be able to get feedback and vital information from the experiences of others and avoid wasting time duplicating research or mistakes.

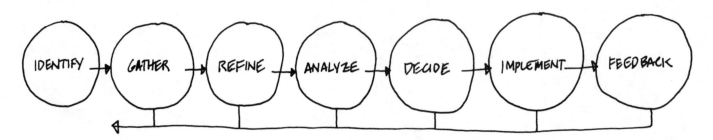

PROJECT DEVELOPMENT Thus, no matter what the project is, the architect generally goes through the same basic steps. The development of an architectural design follows a fairly standard and well-developed process. By adhering to the sequence noted below, the architect can be sure of creating a design that meets the client's financial and emotional needs, as well as achieving the practical purposes the architectural project was designed for.

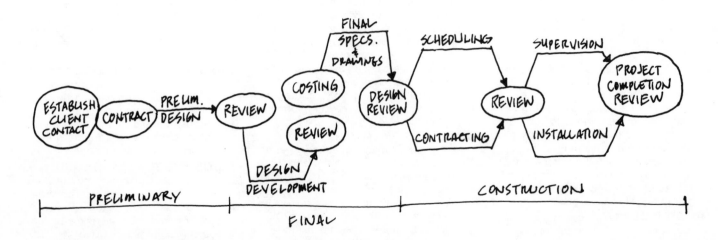

CREATIVITY

GETTING IDEAS Ideas are crucial to any creative field—and that applies as much to architecture as it does to literature and fine art. The architect who is unable to come up with good new ideas is little more than a draftsman, recyling the same old stuff over and over again.

■ That doesn't mean, of course, that everything the professional architect does must be totally original. Truly new ideas are extremely rare. The best work isn't done by those who try to find the brand-new, never-done idea; it's done by those who are able to combine old approaches in new and creative ways.

STEPS FOR GETTING IDEAS

■ Each new project brings its own challenges. The architect must approach it without preconceptions, willing to cast aside old notions and get to work on the job at hand.

■ Each time the architect faces a new project, he or she also faces the exciting task of generating some new ideas. That effort can be awesome, and many would-be architects have fallen by the wayside.

■ That needn't be the case, though. The brain is like a computer. If you, the operator, can learn which buttons to push, and when to push them, you'll be able to proceed through the task of generating ideas just like clockwork. Here are the steps to take:

DEFINE THE PROBLEM Before you can really deal with the new project, you should define the problem. Put down in writing precisely what needs to be resolved.

■ As you take this step, be certain that you are stating the *real* problem. Sometimes people are misled by preconceived notions; they think they know in advance what they're trying to resolve and they don't give this step of the process the amount of effort that it really needs.

GET THE FACTS This is the time to be analytical rather than creative. Ask these questions:

■ What exactly does the client need?

■ How much money is there to work with?

■ What will the building be used for?

■ How have other professionals dealt with similar problems in the past?

STAY OPEN-MINDED Once you have the answers to the questions in the previous step, your first reaction will be to jump to some conclusions. But the immediate solutions the mind first comes up with are not necessarily the best ones.

■ So, keep an open mind. Don't settle on a final solution at this point. At the same time, don't reject any ideas you get. Write them down and defer judgment.

SELECT YOUR MENTAL APPROACH

If you're working with a group, brainstorm possible solutions. Here are some good steps:

■ Clearly state your purpose.

■ Give everyone a chance to throw out ideas.

■ Have someone write *all* the ideas down on the blackboard or a piece of paper.

■ Don't make judgments on any of the ideas during the brainstorming session. Too many ideas are killed before they have a chance to be born.

If you're working on your own, you'll be following a similar process:

■ Make sure you know what you're going after.

■ Write down all your ideas. It may be helpful to carry a notebook in your pocket to write them down as they come to you.

■ Don't judge any idea when it comes. Hold that step until later. Write them *all* down without judgment.

■ Make sure you put yourself in the kind of setting that will stimulate your ideas on the problem at hand.

■ Don't try to force ideas—that will drive them away. Just let them come at their own speed.

MAKE A DECISION Once you've gone through all the mental process just described, you'll have the data you need to make a decision. It will help you to review what you've already done:

■ How does the idea match the criteria listed?

■ How will it appeal to the client?

■ How will it fit with the use the building will be put to?

■ How does it appeal to you aesthetically?

■ If your idea can give satisfactory answers to those questions, you probably have a creative approach that gives a workable (and hopefully exciting) solution to the problem.

IMPLEMENT YOUR IDEA
Good ideas are worthless unless they are made concrete. Make your idea become a reality by getting to work and applying it through renderings, drawings, and plans.

CONSTRUCTION COMMUNICATION

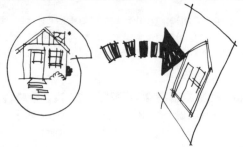

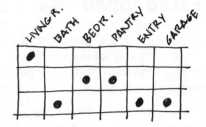

■ Before your design can become a reality, you have to communicate it to the people who will be doing the actual construction. This is done with a set of drawings that depict exactly how the structure is to be built. With those drawings, they'll be able to transform the ideas into actuality.

■ In their final form, these drawings are rendered in pen and ink on vellum. They are then reproduced into multiple sets on blueprint paper.

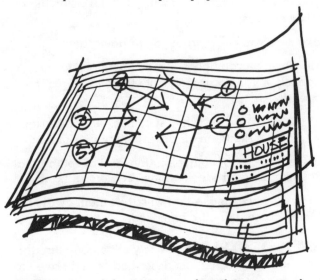

■ Every set of drawings needs to have a standardized system of sizes, lettering, dimensions, and titling. The keys are clarity, legibility, understandability. It may be helpful to consider the contractor as a creature from outer space—and if you fail to communicate effectively you may be attacked!

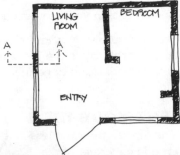

FLOOR PLANS
These show the layout of the rooms, clarifying their relationship to one another. Floor plans are the basic reference point for the entire set of drawings. They will be used in the estimating, scheduling, and actual construction of the building.

SCHEDULES
The schedule indicates the parts of the building that are not part of the structure itself but are nonetheless vitally important. Each different part will have its own schedule. Examples are such things as room finishes and specific kinds of doors or windows.

■ The schedule for each item will specify what the item entails, including the actual materials that will be needed.

■ To be complete, each schedule must indicate the relationship of that section of the building to the remainder of the building; this is done by indicating it's correlation to other drawings.

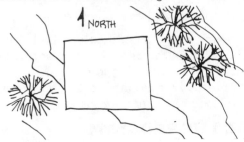

SITE PLAN
This shows the location of the building and its relationship to the land. Outdoor amenities will also be noted. Included will be legal boundaries, slope (kind and degree), key reference points, and information on drainage, vegetation, and soils. Other information needed for site work should be included, along with details on access to sewer, water, and electrical systems.

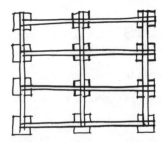

FOUNDATION
Creating the foundation is the first stage of the actual construction of the building. The foundation drawings are basically quite simple: they give necessary details on footings, fireplace footings, anchor bolts, breaks in walls, and drain hoses. These drawings are used to estimate labor and materials for foundation work.

CONSTRUCTION COMMUNICATION

FRAMING Whereas the floor plans tell the builder how to lay out vertical assemblies, the framing plans tell him how to lay out horizontal assemblies. The framing plans give horizontal projections of the building, starting from the lowest level and moving up to the roof. Framing plans indicate key connections and sections. They show the builder how to lay out the floors and roof, with the necessary information on beams, columns, joists, and stiffeners. Details are shown in close-up cuts.

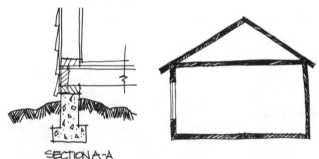

SECTION A-A

SECTIONS When an architect creates his sections, it is as though he took a gigantic vertical cut out of the building so he could look inside. Each section clarifies certain building elements, providing details on such things as stairs, walls, beams, and rooms. The section helps in visualizing spacial relationships.

■ The architect should show as many cross sections as are necessary to give a total view of the building. Elevations and electrical and mechanical systems should be included.

ELEVATIONS These exterior views of the building show the roof, doors, siding, windows, and other such elements from an outside point of view. Elevations illustrate how the structure itself is enclosed—the external surface.

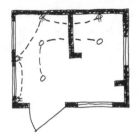

UTILITY PLANS These show a building's electrical and mechanical systems, including the treatment of heating, water, and waste. Even though these details could be shown in the floor plan, they are presented separately to avoid overloading either set of plans with a confusing array of information.

■ Utility work is usually done by licensed subcontractors who specialize in that work.

INTERIOR ELEVATIONS These provide details on the interior elements of the building. An elevation illustrates the surfaces enclosing the interior spaces. Particular attention should be paid to cabinets, millwork, and other such special interior features.

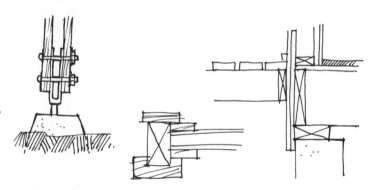

DETAILS Enlargements of the construction of various parts of the building are shown in the details. The details are used where further attention and clarification are needed. An example of a building element that is often detailed is the custom window—such windows must be framed by jobbers in a location separate from the building site.

SPECIFICATIONS
Specifications are drawn to describe the materials that will be used in the building. Included is information on what is needed, where it will be located, what quality is desired (including level of craftsmanship), how it is assembled, and any special characteristics the maker must be aware of.

GRAPHICS

- The architect uses graphics at two vital stages of a design: First, the rough sketches that help develop the design, analyze the problem, and define the context. Second, the more formal drawings that show the future structure in more detail. This second use of graphics lists information on the space, relationships, activities, and system requirements.

KEY POINTS

- Graphics are part and parcel of an architect's work. Graphic skills enable an architect to express ideas in an understandable manner.

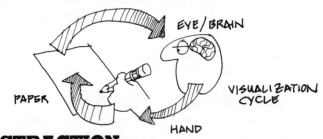

ABSTRACTION

- Architectural graphics should be kept abstract. A simple, general form is easier to handle. If the architect tries to become too detailed too soon, neither the architect nor the client will be able to see the forest for the trees. General information must be evaluated before specific details can be developed.

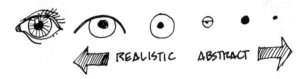

COMMUNICATION

- Graphics are a major element of communication—an important part of the communication process. The architect uses graphics, in the form of drawings, to communicate with himself, first, to help understand and develop the ideas that come from within.

EVOLUTION

- The designer must allow for evolution. Ideas are not static—they evolve. Constantly. As the architect thinks and sketches, new ideas will come to mind. He will build on these, rejecting some and accepting others, until the overall plan gains coherency and direction. He will discuss these ideas with clients and colleagues, using both words and pictures.

VISUALIZATION

- Visualization is an essential part of the communication process. Architecture is by definition a highly visual profession. It is not enough to talk about or write about ideas and plans—they must be put in visual form. The architect must effectively *show*:

- **Hierarchy**—level of importance

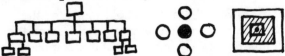

- **Process**—the sequence of action

- **Alternatives**—a priority of design choices

- **Location**—position within space

- **Identifiers**—descriptions of characteristics

- **Size**—the comparison in volume

- **Intensity**—the strength or duration of a particular element

- **Timing**—relationship with time

- **Flow**—the direction of movement

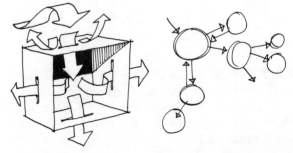

GRAPHICS

KINDS OF GRAPHICS

■ Graphics come in several forms—and each form has its own language. The different languages are all tools of the designer/architect. Each has its own particular influence on the final design.

DIAGRAMS

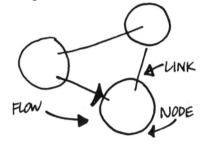

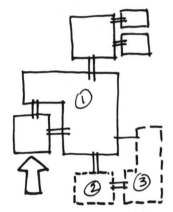

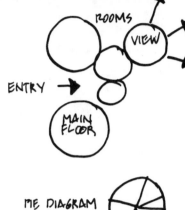

ME DIAGRAM

PLANS

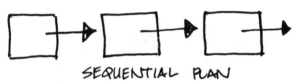

MATRIX

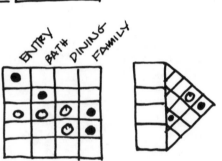

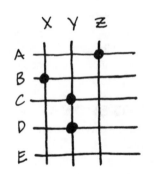

NETWORK

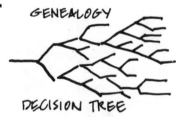

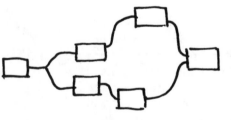

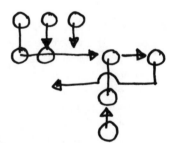

CHART

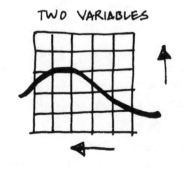

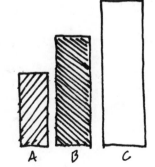

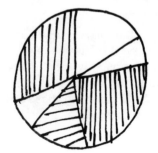

SOLUTIONS

SOLVING PROBLEMS Every architect in the world is a problem solver. The recurring problem is to create aesthetically pleasing architecture while at the same time meeting each client's needs.

■ As a professional architect, you will face such questions as:

How do you develop the ability within yourself to create something that's aesthetically pleasing?

How do you determine the client's true needs?

How do you determine the best use of available funds?

■ The questions are many. How well *you* learn to answer them will determine how good an architect you become. Here are a few points that will help you find the solutions to these kinds of problems.

DESIGN COMPROMISE Recognize that whatever you do, you'll be compromising. It's impossible to find the client who will give you free rein in developing your design. It's equally impossible to find the client with an unlimited bankroll. The result is that you'll have to compromise what you think would be wonderful to do with what you'll actually be able to do. Compromises are necessary, but they must be done with wisdom.

HUMAN RESPONSE Response is the user's reaction to his environment, and is always subjective. But the architect can have an influence on how the user responds. In fact, good design *means* that elements have been arranged in such a way that the user's potential response has been evaluated in advance.

■ One thing that will help you evaluate response is to determine what people are comfortable with. For instance, most of us aren't willing to carry on private conversations in nonprivate settings. Designers of offices should keep that in mind. Many elements come together to bring about the response the user will have. Such factors as lighting, vibration, acoustics, air circulation, and room arrangement should be considered.

■ People often have particular responses to interior environments. They receive cues through the senses and automatically react in social and psychological patterns. (An example is hushed behavior in a cathedral.) Knowing these patterns and using them can be beneficial to an architect.

LEVELS Every element of a design can serve several functions. The same design can work equally well on several different levels. Recognize the many tiers in each segment of a particular building. A bedroom, for example, might be used for sleeping at night, reading or other hobbies during the day, quiet conversation in the evening.

GESTALT The Germans have given us many invaluable concepts, and one of them is *gestalt*. *Gestalt* means:

1. **THE PARTS** of a design solution may be considered, analyzed, and evaluated as distinct components and separate elements.

2. **THE RELATIONSHIP** between the parts is an important to the whole as the parts themselves.

3. **THE WHOLE** of a design solution is different from and *greater* than the sum of its parts. Thus a need for two levels of designing, one the particular and one the general. Both are incomplete without the other.

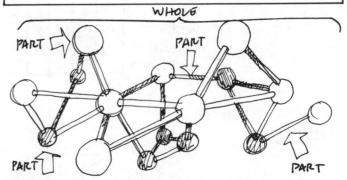

SAFE All design should meet the SAFE criteria—and using that criteria will prove to be an effective problem-solving technique. What is SAFE? It says that all design should be **S**imple, **A**ppropriate, **F**unctional, and **E**conomical.

■ **S**imple means the design should do what's needed with no additional muss or fuss. It should *do*, but not *overdo*.

■ **A**ppropriate means the design should meet the need at hand. It should effectively deal with the issues that need to be considered, and only those.

■ **F**unctional means the design should *work*. It should do what needs to be done.

■ **E**conomical means that the design should be workable in terms of the available money, time, and materials.

■ Frank Lloyd Wright said, "The human race built most nobly when limitations were greatest and, therefore, when most was required of imagination in order to build at all. Limitations seem to have always been the best friends of architecture."

■ Every architect must work with limitations. No one has unlimited budget with unlimited license to do as he or she pleases. Limitations give the architect the opportunity to create something unique in response to a critical need. Consider these examples of architectural responses to limitations:

HIERARCHY OF SPACE

A Jewish temple at the time of Christ, Herod's Temple, gives a good example of how architecture can be designed to provide a hierarchy of space. The temple had the following hierarchy, with each space leading from the previous one:

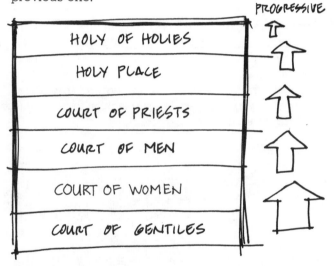

WASTE DISPOSAL

It is reported that some Polynesian people had a workable solution for waste disposal. The solution was to erect outhouses at the end of pier-like structures which jutted out over the water. The islanders would walk out to the outhouse to relieve themselves, and marine organisms recycled the waste through the environment. It was a good

solution. But the islands' populations grew to the point that the old system couldn't keep up. New designs had to be developed.

WIND

People who live in extremely windy areas must have homes capable of withstanding the wind's pressure. French Normandy was settled by sailors who had had experience with the strong winds at sea. They designed their homes so that the end facing the wind resembled the hull of a ship turned upside down.

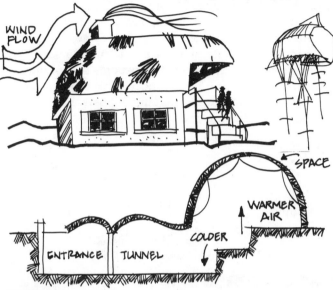

COLD

How do you survive comfortably in a cold, snowy climate? Build an igloo. The entrance is a long curved tunnel which wreaks havoc on drafts. The floor of the main dwelling place is higher than the entrance—another factor that makes the igloo warm.

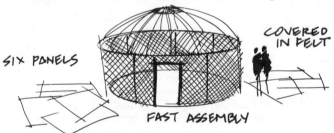

PORTABILITY

The problem here is the need for a suitable structure that is also easily moved. The Mongol Yurt is an excellent example of a solution to this problem.

POLYGAMOUS FAMILIES

In certain areas of the world it is legal and customary for a man to have several wives. The problem is this: how can each of his separate families maintain their privacy and still have easy access to the husband and father?

SPACE

■ Space is what architecture is all about. The architect's job can be simply stated as the manipulation of the forms, patterns, and textures of space. His or her ability is judged by how effectively the available space is molded and structured.

THE HUMAN UNIT In all kinds of space, the human unit is the definer of spatial measurement. The measure, the definition, the structure, the utilization—all is done according to human size. It's the size of the human body that becomes our standard for the architectural use of space. This applies to all forms of that space: inside, outside, personal, public, open, and closed.

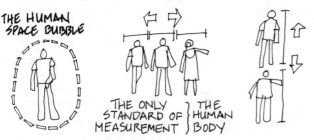

THE HUMAN SPACE BUBBLE

THE ONLY STANDARD OF MEASUREMENT } THE HUMAN BODY

SPATIAL DEFINERS The architect is able to put to use many kinds of definers. These are what divide one unit of space from another. Examples of definers are walls, hedges, sidewalks, trees, flags.

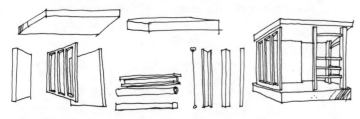

BOUNDARIES Define the space, dividing what's in from what's out, what's up from what's down.

PROPORTIONS Since the human body must interface with every form of architecture, that is the size that determines proportion. The vital question always is: What reactions will the proportions create? Large spaces may create a feeling of awe. Small spaces may convey a cramped feeling.

AFFECTORS The architect can use many elements to affect a person's perception of space.

■ Colors and textures *define* and *frame* the space

■ Warm colors and soft textures create a *warm* environment

■ Cold colors and harsh textures create a *cold* environment

■ Reflective surfaces *enlarge* the space

■ Dull and dark surfaces *reduce* the space

■ Free-standing elements such as furniture or plants, *direct* the space

■ Horizontal elements *elongate* the space

■ Vertical elements *heighten* the space

■ Chaotic use of elements make an ill-defined, *uncertain* space

■ Coordinated elements create a *unified* space

SCALE People relate everything in their environment to themselves. The scale of measure we invariably use is ourself. Even without meaning to, we compare new things with things we know. And we know nothing better than the feel and frame of our own bodies. Everything in architecture is designed to human size, to human scale.

FLOW Buildings are not static but are dynamic. They are not designed to be stiff and inflexible. There will always be motion, movement, change within them.

 ANYTHING FLOWING THROUGH A BUILDING GOES THROUGH A MODIFICATION AND TRANSFORMATION

■ There are several forms of flow that virtually every building will experience. The flowing movements must be considered in the design of the building. For instance, material, information, people, light, air, energy—all these will move through the building in a vibrant way.

EVOLUTION OF SPACE Every development of space goes through several evolutionary steps. Architects can take the design approach they're most comfortable with—yet they'll still take their design through the same evolution. They'll move from general principles to beginning ideas; then from beginning ideas to specific applications.

■ Here are the basic stages every architect goes through:

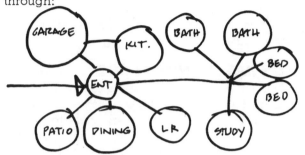

1. Define the units that will work together to create the whole: Diagram.

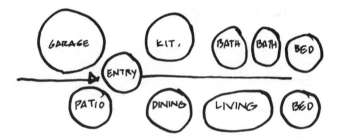

2. Determine the best relationship of the units: See each unit in its context.

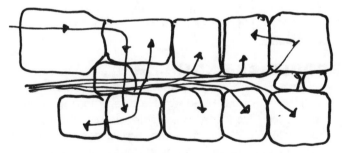

3. Decide on the best size and shape of each unit: Keep in mind the purpose of each.

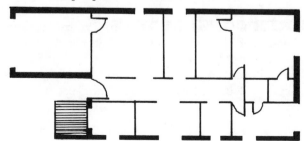

4. Refine the design that's been created: Make a formal drawing showing all details.

QUESTIONS The practice of architecture is the process of finding answers to questions. When no questions remain, the architect's job is done. Sometimes that occurs before the architect even starts—which is probably a signal that a new architect should be called in.

■ The questions must be meaningful. They must be searching. If the questions are trite, the answers will be trite, and the architectural design will also be trite. Sometimes it's harder to find the questions than it is to find the answers. Yet they're incredibly crucial. Those questions could well determine the direction and quality of the entire project. Whenever a new project is faced, the architect should ask himself or herself the following questions (among others, of course):

■ What is the main purpose of this building?

■ How will this building relate to other buildings in the environment?

■ What is the optimal flow through the building?

■ Is the flow for people the same as for things?

■ Does the building have to meet any special requirements?

■ Have the mechanical elements of the building been considered as integral parts of the building—the heating, cooling, plumbing, and so forth?

■ Have secondary uses of the building been considered as integral parts of the buildings—such things as maintenance, repair, visitors, and so forth?

■ Does the building create the right mood or feeling?

■ Have the proper materials been used in the development of the building? Are they at the same time the most economical and the most functional?

■ Have all budget restrictions been kept in mind in the design of the building?

■ Have the client's special needs been respected?

■ Have the building's particular location and climate been given adequate consideration?

■ Do I, the architect, have an overall intent in my design of the building, giving an overall unity to the design?

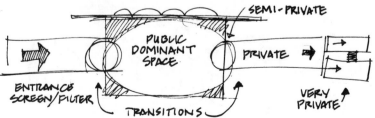

■ Each part of the building has its own place in the hierarchy. The architect must consider the use and purpose of each space and design accordingly.

CONSULTANTS

■ Creating a building requires expertise in a thousand different areas, and the architect can't do it all. Specialization becomes more necessary as our buildings become more complex—and the architect must rely increasingly on outside consulting experts.

■ But it isn't a case of simple reliance—the architect is the team leader who brings many diverse elements together to produce a harmonious whole.

■ To achieve this, the architect must have a working knowledge of all the different disciplines that come together to make up a functional building. An understanding of the basic principles and requirements involved is essential.

STRUCTURAL ENGINEER This expert is concerned with the stability of the building and deals with; loads, stresses, climatic and environmental conditions, strength of materials, cost-to-benefit ratios, building functions, special equipment requirements, special functional requirements, environmental influences, support requirements, new materials and their applications, requirements, and costs.

MECHANICAL ENGINEER The mechanical engineer deals with a wide variety of building systems; mechanical requirements can become quite complex. For example, he or she is concerned with; air conditioning, heating, ventilation, electrical systems, water systems, sanitary systems, and drainage systems.

ELECTRICAL ENGINEER This consultant can help with the electricity and light needed to make the building function. Such things as potential power consumption, equipment requirements, outlet and switching locations, and so forth must be taken into consideration.

LIGHTING CONSULTANT Light is closely related to both economic and aesthetic concerns. The lighting consultant must consider the *use* of the lighting. He or she can help the architect determine how many foot-candles of light are needed for each area of the building, the work requirements for each area, the range of each fixture, the quality and quantity of the lighting being considered, and the safety and security requirements of the building.

INTERIOR DESIGNER The interior designer will both specify and buy the interior furnishings of the building. The interior designer is dealing with the environment where people spend most of their time. This designer, then, is concerned with the relationship of space to people. He or she deals with form, texture, color, and patterns, and uses those elements to determine the best furniture, accessories, and other interior materials for the building.

LANDSCAPE ARCHITECT A building is not an isolated element in space but is intimately connected with living earth. Landscape architecture is environmental architecture, making certain the building coordinates well with its environmental setting. Included elements are; outdoor furniture, lighting, plants, containers and receptacles, and ground surfaces.

GRAPHIC DESIGNER This consultant can be used to enhance the visual image of the building with such things as signage, both directional and informational, environmental graphics, building identification, publications relating to the building, and specialized graphics, such as exhibits, restaurant and bank graphics.

FINE ARTISTS While most other consultants juggle aesthetic and practical concerns, the fine artist is usually free to pursue beauty alone. Such elements as paintings and sculpture help make a building worth living in and provide an important final touch to a design.

ACOUSTICS ENGINEER The acoustics engineer deals with the effects of sound on those who will be using the building. He or she manipulates sound (and its undesirable side, noise) to create the most pleasing, workable atmosphere possible, and is also concerned with the creation and transmission of sound, as in an auditorium, gymnasium, classroom, lecture hall, or theatre.

OTHER CONSULTANTS The architect may need to call in many other consultants, depending on the needs of the design and use of the building. Such consultants may include estimators, transportation experts, doctors, lawyers, historians, sociologists, and so on.

■ The more specialized the building is, the more specialized its design will need to be and the more dependent on specialists you become.

CONSULTANTS
(SPECIALISTS)

ARCHITECT
(GENERALIST)

ARCHITECTURAL BUSINESS

- As a professional architect you can work in several kinds of businesses. These range from being your own boss to working for a huge corporation. Which one you choose depends on your own range of skills and abilities, as well as your wishes and desires.

SOLE PROPRIETORSHIP This is the most common type of architectural business. It's the simplest form of the business—you are your own boss. You are responsible for everything in the business, from the bookkeeping to the coffee-making to the correspondence. You can get others to help you, of course, but in the end you are the one who's responsible.

- In the sole proprietorship, you, the owner of the business, get all the profits. You also get all the liabilities and losses.

PARTNERSHIP This is the result of a legal agreement between two or more people. The partners share equally in the business.

- Partnerships must be entered into with great care. Partners are often liable for their co-partners acts. And the interpersonal relationships involved are often more delicate than those in marriage.

- Participation in a partnership has its advantages, though. Having someone else there can greatly ease the load of ownership. Two heads are involved in making decisions. Two people are involved in keeping the business alive. Two are working at getting more clients and keeping them happy.

ASSOCIATED PRACTICE When two or more firms enter into an agreement to work together, it's called an associated practice. This requires little or no capital to get going—the businesses involved are usually already in existence.

- Often the associated practice has two kinds of individuals in its management: the architect-owner and the architect-associate. The owner gives the associate a base to work from. The associate gives the owner an experienced partner without the hassles of partnership or employees.

- Before joining together in associated practice, those involved should draw up a formal agreement spelling out responsibilities, fee division, and degrees of flexibility.

CORPORATE PRACTICE To form a corporation, the people involved have to employ the services of an attorney, who will organize the corporation according to the laws of the state.

- A corporation is different from the other types of businesses just mentioned in that it has an independent legal existence. It cannot be dissolved at the whim of the owners—it has to conform to legalities.

- One of the most important advantages of a corporation is that it limits the liability of the owners. They are usually not personally responsible for corporate debts. Some tax advantages are also available to corporations. And a corporation can have outside shareholders, who can contribute to the company's coffers by investing their capital.

- Disadvantages: corporations cost considerably more to form; and they may cost more to keep going, mainly because of employee expenses, government regulations, etc.

JOINT VENTURE This is a one-time collaboration of several separate people or companies. All members of the venture are individually and jointly responsible for the completion of the project. The venture has no existence after the job is done.

- A joint venture retains no profits after the completion of the job; and it isn't taxable. Payments are distributed to the individual members in the amounts and on the schedule agreed upon. Workload, work assignments, and the like should all be agreed upon in advance.

- Joint ventures should be started only after a formal letter of agreement has specified the participation of all involved. It should clarify the work and money distribution; work schedule, payment schedule, relationships, and so forth.

EXPANDED PRACTICE As a company grows in clients, it may grow in area of influence as well. First it may grow to other states. To undertake a commission in another state, an architect must first become registered in that state—or must associate with someone who is registered. Working in another state has both legal and tax implications; a good tax attorney should be consulted.

- The company can also go international. There is a great demand for qualified architects in many of the Third World countries. When moving into other areas, architects must carefully familiarize themselves with local culture, tradition, religion, climate, government, and law.

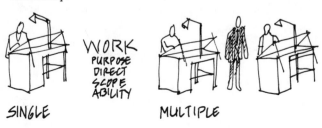

WORK
PURPOSE
DIRECT
SCOPE
ABILITY

SINGLE   MULTIPLE

PROFESSIONALISM

- Architecture is a business. Some architects like to think of themselves as artists only—but they don't last long in the *business*. The most successful architects are those who are able to mesh the artistic with the practical.

- Architecture is like any other business in the world. The professional writer who doesn't keep good books soon loses his shirt. The plumber who isn't able to attract and keep clients soon goes out of business. Doing paperwork, figuring estimates, maintaining records, doing research—it's all a part of the job. True professionals concern themselves with all the details of their work and seek to do all aspects equally well.

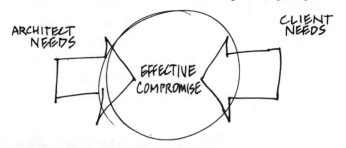

THE BIG PROBLEM

- There's another problem all architects must face: they are expected to do the best job possible and still please the client. That's probably the biggest problem in the business—matching the aesthetic needs of the job with the client's needs and financial restraints. The professional architect diligently seeks that match in every job he or she undertakes.

PROFESSIONAL IMAGE

- An architect's image is at stake in all he or she does. How well the client's expectations are met will determine whether the architect is viewed as a professional, an amateur, or a fraud. The neglect or incompetence of a few in the field can give everyone a bad name. Testing by national organizations and licensing by states aids the image; but each individual architect must build on that image by professional performance. Ultimately, the architect's environmental impact, as well as his or her level of involvement and financial remuneration, is determined by the professional image projected.

FEES

- Architects receive different kinds of payment for different kinds of work. The payment is generally given as a percentage of the total cost of erecting the building.

PERCENTAGES
Fees vary from time to time and from place to place, but the generally accepted fees are these:

- Remodeling 10%

- Residential 10%-12%

- Commercial Construction 6%-7%

BILLING SCHEDULE

5%	To begin project
10%	Schematics
15%	Design Development
50%	Construction Documents (plans and specs.)
5%	Bid Phase
15%	Construction Administration
100%	of Total fee (based on "Percentages")

PROFESSIONALISM

WORKING WITH THE CLIENT

■ The seven steps of working with a client will demonstrate how an architect can successfully handle this aspect of his business:

CONTACT Your first contact with a client may be by letter or by telephone. Tell the client who you are and what you can do to meet his or her needs.

INTERVIEW The next step is to meet each other in an interview. There you convince the client that you can fulfill his or her needs.

RAPPORT It's crucial in the interview to establish a rapport with the client. Show that you *understand* what he or she needs. Help the client see that you'll be able to work well together.

CREDIBILITY You need to establish your ability to fulfill your promises. Here's where your portfolio and resume come in. They show the client that you have experience, ability, and professional recognition.

UNDERSTANDING Once the client has agreed to work with you, you both need to come to an understanding. Define who will do what in the relationship. Be specific. Discuss the purpose of the project, the deadlines, the payment, and other such items.

COMMITMENT Now that you've reached an understanding, draw up an agreement which spells out your commitment to each other. It's often a good idea to have the client sign a simple contract that indicates he or she wants your services and is willing to pay for them. Keep a copy of that contract—you probably won't need it again, but it will be nice to have if you *do* need it.

REVIEW Once you get started on the job, you'll want to see the client periodically to review the progress and expectations of the job. Give the client feedback about your work and get feedback on the client's feelings.

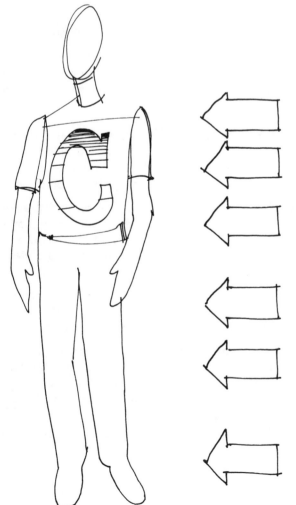

FITTING THE CLIENT

■ Remember that the client is a unique individual with needs and concerns different from those of anyone else you've ever worked with. Keep in mind the critical elements of those needs:

PHYSICAL: What physical needs must the building meet?

EMOTIONAL: How emotionally involved is the client? What emotional hang-ups does he or she bring to the job?

INTELLECTUAL: How does the client intellectually view the process and product of architectural design? How easily does he or she accept new concepts and ideas?

MOTIVATIONAL: What are the client's inner reasons and motivations for seeking the architectural design? How deep-seated are those reasons?

EXPECTATIONAL: What kind of design does the client hope to end up with? How set are those hopes? How crucial is it that you meet those expectations—or could they be replaced with something else?

ECONOMICAL: What economical constraints has the client set? What effect will the limitation of money have on the final design? Do the expectations match the amount of money that's available?

GETTING A JOB

■ Training does little good if you can't get a job with it. And getting that job is in some ways as much a skill as being able to design brilliantly. It involves being able to put together an application that will impress the prospective employer—and it involves impressing the employer in a face-to-face interview.

■ Some beginning architects expect to go right to work with their most highly developed skills. This is generally a mistake. An apprenticeship must first be served. Most beginners, despite their background and training, will start with a firm as draftsmen. Only after they prove themselves there—both in ability and in dependability—will they be given more difficult assignments.

THE INTERN-ARCHITECT DEVELOPMENT PROGRAM

■ This program sets minimum standards which aspiring architects must meet. To qualify, you must have five years of professional education, culminating in a degree. Then comes three years practical training.

WORK EXPERIENCE Training experience enjoyed while still in school may be applied toward the three years of postgraduate training. For example:

■ work experience in a registered architect's office (no limit to how much)
■ work experience in construction under the supervision of a registered architect (only two years of this experience may apply)
■ work experience in construction *not* under the supervision of a registered architect (only one year may apply).

QUALIFYING TESTS In addition to the Intern-Architect Development Program, a prospective architect must pass the tests of the National Council of Architectural Registration Boards. The Qualifying Test runs for nine hours and breaks down like this:

■ **Section A:** Architectural History (2 hours)
■ **Section B:** Structural Technology (3 hours)
■ **Section C:** Materials and Methods of Construction (2 hours)
■ **Section D:** Environmental Controls and Systems (2 hours)

■ Once a person has passed the Qualifying Test, he may take the Professional Examination:

■ **Section A:** Site-planning and Design (one day for 12 hours)
■ **Section B:** Multiple Choice Test, Four Parts (two days for a total of 16 hours)

Part 1—Environmental Analysis
Part 2—Architectural Programming
Part 3—Design and Technology
Part 4—Construction

THE EMPLOYER

■ When you seek a job, you have a major hurdle to cross—the employer. If you can please the employer you have the job. If you can't, you're back on the street looking elsewhere. There's a key you can use in trying to please the employer: find out what he or she needs and show how you can meet those needs.

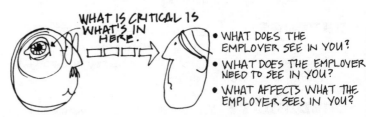

WHAT IS CRITICAL IS WHAT'S IN HERE.

• WHAT DOES THE EMPLOYER SEE IN YOU?
• WHAT DOES THE EMPLOYER NEED TO SEE IN YOU?
• WHAT AFFECTS WHAT THE EMPLOYER SEES IN YOU?

SEE THEIR POINT OF VIEW How do you know an employer's needs? Start by doing some homework. See what kinds of jobs he or she takes on. Then read the job description very carefully. Finally, when you go in for the interview, make sure that you listen to what the employer has to say.

■ Too often applicants spend all their time describing how wonderful they are, without bothering to find out that all that wonderfulness doesn't fit at all with what the employer needs.

FIRST IMPRESSIONS The first impression is hard to escape. When you go the interview, the employer is going to make an immediate judgment. How do you ensure a favorable impression?

■ The answer is not difficult. Simply look the part. *Look* like the kind of person you think the employer wants and you'll be two steps ahead of the competition. Dress to impress. Be groomed in such a way that the employer will think you're the person for the job.

■ You also need to *talk* the part. Know what the business is about. Know what architectural terminology is, when to use it, and when not to use it.

■ In addition to your person, the prospective employer is going to judge you by two other things—the *resume* and the *portfolio*. The resume will give your background; and the portfolio will show what kind of work you've done in the past.

RESUME

■ The resume is a typed sheet giving a concise overview of your background. Make sure it's up-to-date and professional in appearance. You may want to get an english teacher or a skilled friend to help you with the spelling, grammar, punctuation, and syntax.

■ Every resume is different. They're as individual as fingerprints. But every one can follow the same general outline. In preparing your resume, be sure to keep your audience in mind. If you want to get a job teaching architecture, be sure to emphasize your teaching experience. If you want to get a job designing, be sure to emphasize your practical experience. As you prepare the resume, keep in mind who will be reading it. Consider what the prospective employer will be looking for, and highlight those things.

■ Here are the elements that every resume will contain:

PERSONAL List your name and address and telephone number. When you were born, whether or not you're married, how many kids you have. How healthy you are (unless you're unhealthy—then you might want to leave out this part!).

EDUCATION Where you graduated from high school, and when. When and where you graduated from college. What your major and minor were. If you ended up with a good grade-point average, what it was. Mention any courses you took that have particular bearing on the job in question (not too many). Mention any special seminars or training workshops you attended. Remember to mention only things that have a bearing on the job you're trying to get; emphasize the education that will boost your chances.

WORK EXPERIENCE Note the job you have now, complete with your duties and salary, and work backwards. Part-time and summer jobs don't deserve any mention—unless they're related to architecture. Don't forget to include a note about supervisory duties—those show that your previous employer thought highly of you.

OTHER EXPERIENCE If you've had other experience, perhaps in church or community service, that shows you're an exceptional person or that relates to architecture, include it under this heading.

AWARDS AND MEMBERSHIPS Impressive things that indicate excellence and involvement in various related activities.

REFERENCES There are two approaches you can use here. One is to say, "References provided upon request." The second, and better, approach, is simply to list people who can vouch for your ability and/or trustworthiness. Contact several people in advance and ask if you can note them as references. Good choices are former employers who liked your work, your clergyman, a community leader, a local businessman, and the like. These people will give added credibility to your application—and to you.

OTHER ITEMS Here you can put your career goals or your personal interests and hobbies. These are really unnecessary unless: (1) you want to show the potential employer that you have a broad range of interests; (2) your interests will raise your chances of getting the job.

You may have noted a dilemma in the above section: the employer is going to evaluate you on the basis of your past experience, and you don't have any in the field. This is your first job—how can you be expected to have experience?

The army recruiter will give you one solution: join the army and get the experience, then you can get the job. But that answer isn't right for most of us.

Here's a better solution, a way to break out of the vicious circle of "No experience? Sorry, no job!" and "But if I can't get a job how do I get experience?" Try this: while you're still in school, contact one or two of the architectural firms in the area. Tell them that you want to get a little experience—that you'll help them out *for free*. They'll probably give you all the junk jobs (like emptying the trash), but that doesn't matter. Because at the same time you'll be getting some experience in a real work situation. And you can put that experience down on your resume.

Another approach that works is to do some free architectural renderings for your family and friends. Or, if you can, enter into bidding for jobs; those will give you experience both in bidding and in rendering—but if by chance you get the job, you'd better be ready to perform!

PORTFOLIO

■ The portfolio is probably even more important than the resume. The resume will *tell* what you've done; but the portfolio will *show* it. It will give the prospective employer (or client) an actual look at what you can do.

WHAT DOES THE PORTFOLIO INCLUDE?
For starters, put in the very best examples of your work. Include a wide variety of things—renderings, floor plans, photos of models, and so forth. Pick the very best things you can find: the employer isn't particularly interested in seeing your bad stuff, to learn how far you've come. He or she only wants to know how good you are now.

■ Be sure to tailor-make the portfolio to the needs of the employer. If he or she specializes in commercial buildings, it would be a mistake to include even your very best work in residential design.

■ Ten to twenty pieces is generally sufficient for a good portfolio. Too few won't give the employer a good enough feel for what you can do, too many will be overwhelming.

■ One important thing for any beginning architect to include is a complete set of working drawings. Your first job will probably be as a draftsman, and the employer wants to know your abilities in that area.

CONTACT COMMUNICATION

■ Before you as an architect, can use your skills and training, you must have *clients* to use them with. The ability to get clients is virtually as important as the ability to design a workable building. In essence, an architect must also be a salesman. The product: yourself and your abilities. As an architect, you can use several proven ways for selling yourself and getting clients:

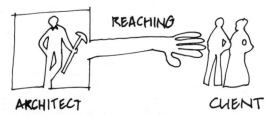

BROCHURE/PORTFOLIO The brochure is a printed and folded (or stapled) booklet describing your background and the jobs you've done successfully in the past. Include specific projects and the names of clients. It should be professionally written, photographed, and printed. Color costs a lot more than black and white to produce, but the difference in the final product can make the cost well worth it.

■ The portfolio is much like the brochure—but rather than have it mass produced, you'll create only one portfolio. It should include examples of your drawings at all stages (but especially at the final stage), as well as photographs of your representative buildings or other projects that have been completed.

PROPOSALS The proposal is a written document that you'll give to the client; it suggests what you would do if you were chosen to design a specific project the client has in mind.

■ The successful proposal will show the client that you have a good feel for what he or she needs; break the project down into its individual tasks; list which of your staff members will be assigned to which parts of the job; show why you are qualified to do the job; establish cost and completion schedules; and propose payment arrangements.

PRESS RELEASES Getting your name featured in the newspaper is a good sales tool. There are several things that might warrant an article or notice in the paper. For example, if you begin a large or unusual project, win an award, or move to a new location, you might want to send out a press release. Make it well-written and interesting, and be sure to include all the pertinent facts and photos if any. Then send the release to local newspapers.

NEWSLETTERS Periodically you can send out a newsletter discussing your current projects; send copies to clients and potential clients. Make it as interesting as possible; make sure it shows how your services could be valuable to the prospective client.

REPORTS A report is assigned by the client—and paid for by him too! A report contains much the same information as that included in a proposal. Except, of course, the proposal is done on speculation and the report has been requested. The report can be a real selling tool; often the client will use it to evaluate the architect as well as to get more details about his project.

LETTERS You can use a letter to introduce yourself to the client, or you can use it to follow up on previous communications. Letters that are clean, clear, to the point, and specific do much to raise the architect's image in the client's mind.

EXHIBITS An exhibit is predominantly *visual*, and that applies to the writing as well as to the photos and drawings. Mock layouts are interesting elements to be considered as part of an exhibit, as are schedules, renderings, photographs, and materials samples.

DIRECT MAILINGS Direct mailing is similar to a personal letter, only done on a mass scale. Create a list of people who might be interested in your services, and send them a letter of introduction or a brochure. Make the mailing brief, easy to understand, relevant, and visually impressive.

AUDIO-VISUAL PRESENTATIONS This category includes everything from slide presentations with (or even without) a tape-recorded script to a full-scale motion picture. The first time you produce such a presentation you'll probably learn so much that you'll want to do it over, if you have the funds.

■ The basic steps of preparing an audio-visual presentation:

- ■ Thumbnails
- ■ Script
- ■ Visuals
- ■ Recording
- ■ Coordination of visuals with recording

INFORMATION

- Flow of information is an important aspect of architecture. The architect doesn't sit alone in an office day after day working on little private plans; on the contrary, architects are constantly involved with other people, always on the look-out for new ideas and new solutions to problems. They are always in the process of *becoming* better architects, and information is essential to that process. They must keep pace with the latest developments in the field.

- Architects can't simply copy the work of others yet at the same time, they cannot rely solely on themselves. They must be both self-reliant and open to influence from others. This is the role of *information*.

- To get all the ideas in this book, you'd have to go to literally dozens of other sources. And perhaps you should! After you've mastered these concepts, you'll be ready to seek even greater understanding. That can be found by reading more and more in the field—and practicing more and more of what you learn. The subject of architecture is very complex. Learning everything there is to know about it is a lifetime project. The time to start, of course, is now!

INFORMATION SOURCES Below is a list of good sources of information on architecture. The list is by no means exhaustive, but these books and periodicals will give you a start on some sources that will help you.

- As you consider the books listed here, remember it is possible to get some good ideas from books not written specifically on architecture. Catalogues for related areas, photo encyclopedias, and visually oriented books of all kinds may be helpful.

PERIODICALS

Abitare
AIA Journal
Architectural Design, Cost and Data
Architectural Record
Building Design and Construction
Contract Interiors
Domus
Forms and Surfaces
Landscape Architecture
Progressive Architecture

BOOKS

Architecture: City Sense
Theo Crosby
Van Nostrand Reinhold

How Buildings Work: The Natural Order of Architecture
Edward Allen
Oxford University Press

Architectural Graphics
Frank Ching
Van Nostrand Reinhold

Architecture: Action and Plan
Peter Cook
Van Nostrand Reinhold

Techniques of Successful Practice for Architects and Engineers
William B. Foxhall
Architectural Record

The Elements of Structure
W. Morgan
Pitman Publishing

Graphic History of Architecture
John Mansbridge
Viking Press

Space, Time, and Architecture
S. Giedron
Harvard University Press

Architectural Styles
Herbert Pothron
Viking Press

Archigram
Peter Cook
Praeger Publishers

Exterior Design in Architecture
Yoshonoku Ashthard
Van Nostrand Reinhold

Form, Function and Design
Paul Jacques Grillo
Dover

Houses Architects Design for Themselves
Walter F. Wagner Jr.
Architectural Record

Architecture: Form, Space and Order
Francis D. K. Ching
Van Nostrand Reinhold

Architecture Today and Tomorrow
C. Jones
McGraw-Hill

REFERENCES

The Timeless Way of Building and a Pattern Language
Christopher Alexander
Oxford University Press

Working Drawing Handbook a Guide for Architects and Builders
Robert C. McHugh
Van Nostrand Reinhold

Graphic Problem Solving for Architects and Builders
Paul Laseau
Van Nostrand Reinhold

Energy-Efficient Buildings
Walter F. Wagner Jr.
Architectural Record

Architectural and Interior Models
Sanford Hotauser
Van Nostrand Reinhold

Architectural Graphic Standards
Ramsey and Sleeper
Wiley and Sons

Graphics for Architecture
Kevin Forseth
Van Nostrand Reinhold

Sweets Architectural Catalog File

Architecture: a Profession and a Business
Morris Loprdus
Van Nostrand Reinhold

YOUR NOTES

■ Architecture will only be yours if *you* make it so. This notebook contains hundreds of principles and ideas on architecture; but it is just a start. This basic material will be of real value to you when you immerse yourself, participate in, and become involved with your own learning process. Your notes will reflect your own style, needs, and interests. They will become an extension of this notebook in your own personal style. What does architecture mean to you? What are its most important principles? How does architecture effect your everyday life? Use this opportunity to expand your architectural life.